Not Minding That It Hurts

Ian Carnaby

D1464998

MARTEN
JULIAN

1970 • 2005

Published by
Marten Julian, 69 Highgate, Kendal, Cumbria, LA9 4ED
Tel: 01539 741007

First published in Great Britain 2005

ISBN 0-9546109-7-0

Typeset & Printed in Great Britain by
MTP Media Ltd, Kendal, Cumbria
www.mtp-media.co.uk

Dedicated to my wife Sue,
who disapproves thoroughly but quietly.

Contents

Foreword

Having read and admired Ian Carnaby's work over many years, it was with some trepidation that I approached him soon after the closure of *The Sporting Life* to ask if he might be willing to write an article for my *Dark Horses Annual.* To my delight he agreed, since when he has contributed to my publications on a regular basis and established a loyal following amongst my clients.

Ian is blessed with a special talent. His work has that rare knack of prompting the most emotive of responses in the reader. Somehow he makes you feel nostalgic for an age or time you may never even have known.

It has been a delight to work with Ian over the past few years and I welcome this opportunity to publish a few of his articles, observations and short stories. I hope they give you as much pleasure as they did me when I first read them.

Marten Julian

Introduction

Ian Carnaby, only child and gambler, was born and raised in Southampton, a town for which he still feels great affection. Educated there and later at Cambridge, where he studied Modern Languages and sprint handicaps, he worked in the wine trade for Gilbeys throughout the seventies and was brand manager for Baileys Irish Cream, leaving a few weeks before it became world famous.

Having reported on football for just about every local radio station in the country, and commentated on boxing at Reading Town Hall, where the ring collapsed, he joined BBC Radio in 1982, working with the late Peter Bromley. He was racing correspondent for Robert Maxwell's ill-fated *London Daily News*, learned a bit about television presenting at HTV West and became front man for SIS (Satellite Information Services) soon after its launch in 1987.

This period is remembered chiefly for the arrival of a charming (if puzzled) cleaning lady at his side while he was talking, on air, about Tottenham Hotspur. Eagerly snapped up by Dennis

Norden, this exchange has been seen around the world and dubbed into Italian.

A freelance scribbler and occasional broadcaster since 1991, he has been English correspondent of the *Irish Field* for 17 years, wrote his own troubled, introspective column in the late, lamented *Sporting Life*, and owned a winner or two with Pat Murphy to add to those trained by Gavin Pritchard-Gordon when the world was young.

He likes Italian restaurants, especially in mid-afternoon when the serious people have gone, Southampton leading two-nil with ten seconds left, a little bit of Ella in the night, and the novels of Thomas McGuane.

Ian Carnaby lives quietly with his wife and family in Nailsea, but produces much of his material in the Sawyer's Arms or The Old Duke, a famous jazz pub in Bristol.

Sometimes it shows.

Acknowledgements

The author and publishers are grateful to the following: George Ennor and John Curtis, for their time and expertise in checking the text; Dan and Ric Colebourn for assisting so conscientiously with the research; Gavin McPhail for his superb illustrations and Chris Nicholson for overseeing the project. Stuart Brown, Rebecca Dixon and Steve Dixon are also thanked for their contributions.

one

The Ghosts Of Christmas Past

I was six years old when Halloween won the King George VI Chase for the second time.

My parents, who worked hard for their money and were not gamblers, apart from a few shilling doubles here and there, had made quite an effort that Christmas. I am an only child, so all of the presents were mine. I played with them for an hour or so, and then asked my father to play rummy with me. I liked the faces on the court cards even then; the Jack of Clubs with his sly look, the King of Diamonds' dignity. Many years later the Queen of Spades cost me a lot of money, but she'd been threatening it for a while and I took it well. When I was six, she looked merely prim and correct.

Needless to say, my parents were disappointed when so many brightly wrapped gifts gave best to the fifty-two soldiers in Satan's army, as the elder Steptoe once described a pack of playing cards. Not that they saw it as a defining moment, although they should have done. As far as my father (a canny ex-miner who favoured 33'1 shots trained by E Magner) was concerned, the penny only dropped when New Liskeard won for Eric Cousins at Haydock about ten years later, because that was my first £1 bet. The first £5, £10 and £20 bets all won as well which is a bad thing of course, like winning the first time you visit a casino, because it means they've got you. When I had my first £50 bet, on Whortleberry at Newmarket, it was beaten on the nod.

The family, all three of us, backed Halloween because he was trained by Bill Wightman. In those days people living in Southampton, if they bet at all, tended to follow Wightman or Les Hall, both of whom trained just up the road. If I had to list the best things that have happened to me as a racing journalist, meeting Bill would come top.

Apart from being an outstanding trainer, he is a truly remarkable man, someone who survived a Japanese POW camp, even though his weight went down to 7st 12lb. "There were more deaths as each successive Christmas passed. At the finish we were burying fifteen men a week, a friend every day. The atom bomb was the only thing that saved us – that's for sure. If they hadn't dropped the bomb, thousands more British prisoners would have died."

It is very hard for those under fifty to imagine how racing was broadcast half a century ago. It was gung-ho, enthusiastic stuff, long on enthusiasm and short on reliable detail. I worked as the late Peter Bromley's 'runner' and odds man on BBC Radio for three years from 1982 onwards. Bromley was a very private man whose bark was much worse than his bite, and I liked the way he did his own thing for the BBC, seldom bothering with pressroom chit-chat or even seeking out fellow journalists at all. He was a commentator first and foremost, and made sure the BBC never forgot it. He opened the right door at the right time and called the shots for 40 years.

I once asked him how he'd made it all possible. "Well, no disrespect, but I listened to Raymond Glendenning's commentaries and I thought, by golly, if I can't do better than that, there's no point bothering." Which was fair comment. The difference between sports broadcasting in the fifties and sixties – Peter took over in 1960 – was that you had to get things right. In the fifties, the public was still supposed to feel pleased it was getting anything at all. Now, every single mistake is picked up and shredded by the *Daily Mail*, unless someone else gets there first.

My mother allowed me sixpence on Halloween, which meant going with my Aunt Em to a street corner and waiting for Ern, the Southampton bus inspector who doubled as a bookie's runner, to turn up. The King George was run on December 27th that year, which made things slightly easier because a few buses were running, though I suspect Ern would have been there anyway.

He ferried bets to the wonderfully named Johnny Denton, who should probably have been a riverboat gambler falling slowly and fatally in love with Barbara Stanwyck, but actually ran an office in Brookvale Road. When I was a few years older I peered in through the window and a blonde winked at me. Funny to think what might have happened if I'd stayed around. Forty years on, the wink would do.

My recollection of the radio commentary is hazy, but it was one of the more straightforward ones because Halloween and his old rival Galloway Braes went clear with a mile to travel and Wightman's horse, ridden by Fred Winter, was in front at the last, going on to score by six lengths. Glendenning had obviously committed the Contessa di Sant' Elia's colours to memory, and there were few worries in the Carnaby household from the turn into the straight.

Given my time again (a singularly pointless conversational gambit) I'd have tried to be an actor rather than a sports journalist. Still, I interviewed Bill Wightman for *The Sporting Life* when he retired and I worked with Peter Bromley. These are things I cherish, together with the Vitas Gerulaitis interview for a BBC Radio programme in the eighties, when we wandered around a London hotel looking for a quiet place to record, and finally sat down on the floor in a deserted corridor.

Someone should work out the number of times Gerulaitis was two sets up in a major tennis tournament and still managed to lose. A man of irresistible charm, it transpired that he had often been playing the casinos at 4am the same day. He lived entirely for the moment, accepting that less gifted but more dedicated professionals would often wear him down.

It's a pity Scott Fitzgerald wasn't around at the same time.

Then wear the gold hat, if that will move her;
If you can bounce high, bounce for her too,
Till she cry "Lover, gold-hatted, high-bouncing lover,
I must have you!"

He'd have liked that, Gerulaitis. Be someone's angel for a while. Live fast, die young. I wish I'd known him better.

Afternoon Reflections

I admit to being a sucker for Christmas. I love the build-up, the carols, the first time 'White Christmas' comes on and all the rest of it, although I am not especially religious. I like hearing other people's views, though, so I always invite the Jehovah's Witnesses in and we talk about this and that, and they decline tea, coffee and a shot of Glenmorangie and wander off again, having taken my advice on which houses to avoid, which is most of them.

The last time they were in they asked if I believed in an afterlife, which I do, I suppose, although Lord only knows what you do after the first couple of weeks, when you've seen everyone and apologised. If we're punters, how can we manage without risk? If there are no problems, what will we talk about? If we don't need money, presumably there's no work. And if there's no work, what do we do all day? See? You haven't thought it through at all, have you?

I can't really remember how the topic came up, but I once interviewed the leading independent bookmaker, Stephen Little, and asked him why he didn't believe in an afterlife. "Oh, I don't know," he said. "Just the sheer logistics, I suppose."

Incomparable Arkle – Nearly

I bet steadily all through my school days, and became known for it. When betting offices were introduced there was nothing for Ern to do, except track down an errant number 11 or 14 and give the driver a hard time, and his heart wasn't in it. The old Palladium cinema closed as well, so the next time I saw *The Man From Laramie* was on television, which wasn't the same thing at all.

The Christmas before I went to Cambridge (something of a fluke, incidentally, my English essay about a chap who'd lost the will to live and set off up a bleak mountainside, not giving a bugger about anything, apparently catching the examiners on the right day), Arkle broke down in the King George and never raced again. Boxing Day was on the 27th that year, as well, and there was a general mood of gloom.

People try to compare other steeplechasers with him, but he is clearly out on his own. When he finished second to Stalbridge Colonist in the 1966 Hennessy, with What A Myth close up, he was conceding well over two stones to the pair of them, and they went on to finish second and third in the Gold Cup a few months later. In fact, the only horse you could possibly put up against him would be his flashy stable-companion Flyingbolt, who won the Champion Chase at Cheltenham and then finished third in the Champion Hurdle at the same meeting. People do not realise how much tougher horses were then, or how much more was expected of them, especially in Ireland. Flyingbolt, by the way, was rated only 2lb behind Arkle by Timeform.

Tom Dreaper trained both, of course, as well as the talented grey Owen's Sedge, who was owned by Gregory Peck and won the 1963 Leopardstown Chase. The actor visited the Jockey Club in London just before Christmas 1967, reducing the female staff to a kind of mute, open-mouthed stupefaction. Germaine Greer would have been very annoyed with them. Strangely, when I worked there for a while in 1970, they talked all the time.

Hardly anyone at the Jockey Club seemed to bet, prompting thoughts of eunuchs in bordellos, but in my six months as a graduate trainee I managed to redress the balance. One of my great problems in life has always been the lunch hour. It takes a while to find a small Italian restaurant close to a pub with decent bitter and a betting shop not far away.

I don't mind how early I start work in the morning, and I've been known to sit in darkened offices of an evening, making the most elaborate plans for the following day. But I do like a drop of Barolo and some Sinatra in the afternoon. Decadence without funds is tricky, but there is generally a way of managing it. People have removed me from the payroll for this attitude, and I don't blame them. But, as the years roll by, it seems to matter less.

(Incidentally, lest I forget, and just in case you end up in Shaftesbury Avenue under the non-triers' rule or whatever, go down to Marylebone High Street where it meets Thayer Street and have lunch in the Hellenic Greek restaurant. It's bang opposite a Ladbrokes, and the Greeks generally have good tips from Jeremy Noseda, who's been going there since he was six. If you walk round the corner into Marylebone Lane, you can get an excellent pint in The Golden Eagle, and the phone by the bar works. You could just about fit all of that into an hour although, as an alleged non-trier, you may have to give yourself a few reminders. If you fall back exhausted, just stay in the Hellenic; they're very understanding.)

November Chill

November has always been my favourite month. I like the short days, the chill of the early evening, the promise of Christmas. When I was at Cambridge, where three years passed like three months, I went to the late Newmarket meetings on the bus, eyeing the shop girls in Cherry Hinton, their collars turned up against the cold, on the way home.

When I wrote that preferring rummy to presents as a six-year old was probably a defining moment, I think there were a couple more at Cambridge. The first £20 bet was on a filly called Benita, trained early on by Jack Waugh, though she moved to Henry Cecil as a three-year old and landed quite a gamble for him.

As a juvenile, she ran sixth first time up and was then fancied for a maiden at Lingfield. She was quite a loud whisper in Cambridge, and I had £20 on at 9'4. That was a fair-sized bet for a student more than thirty years ago. It soon became obvious that those in the know at Lingfield were not at all worried about Benita, because a debutante of Staff Ingham's called Abigail Hill was considered a cast-iron certainty. She was evens, I think, or 11'10, and lost lengths at the start before finishing fourth. There is no doubt she was unlucky, and all these years later I wonder if it would have been better had she won.

When I sit and think about it now, I acknowledge that I was never remotely interested in backing horses as a hobby – it had to hurt badly or feel wonderful. I also think that most gamblers spend a lifetime trying to get back to where they started, and very few succeed.

Elsworth – A Grumpy Genius

During my time at the BBC I always worked on Boxing Day. There was something magical about setting out for Kempton with hardly any traffic on the road, though that changed near the course. I happen to know the Sunbury area very well, because I sold drink in the pubs and clubs there during the seventies.

Most of the publicans were interested in racing, so it was just a question of taking the order and then studying the day's cards. I remember with particular affection The Chequers in Isleworth, run by a man called Ken Balls. (I am not making this up.) There was a regular, Norman, who sat at the bar and routinely needed three large vodka and tonics early in the morning to return him to the land of the living following the previous night's excesses.

The strange thing was, he used just one small bottle of Schweppes Tonic, merely adding a few drops as Ken topped up the Smirnoff. On the third one, Norman would suddenly turn to me and say, "Hello, Ian! I didn't see you there" (even though I'd been standing next to him all the time). "Anything good today?"

It was an extraordinary performance, and taught me all about the restorative powers of vodka and tonic, something that Elton John cottoned on to as long ago as 'Goodbye Yellow Brick Road'. One morning, when Norman was back on top form, I asked Ken why he didn't take more Schweppes with it. "He worries about the quinine," he said.

I also visited an Irish pub in Feltham, where they organised a sweep on the Feltham Novices' Chase when there were enough runners. As I say, taking the order was easy, because it was all tied trade – Gilbeys Gin, J & B Whisky, Smirnoff, Hennessy etc. But in the Feltham pub there was a huge bottle of Booth's Gin on optic, with a torn label which had seen better days.

Fearing that the area manager might ask questions, I asked the publican about the Booth's – which, being of a certain age, you will probably recall had a slightly yellowish tinge to it. It transpired that three elderly ladies, who never missed a morning session, invariably called me darling (God, I miss those days), and had trodden the boards in Shaftesbury Avenue, or possibly Windmill Street, always asked for Booth's by name.

"You're supposed to serve Gilbeys, you know," I said to him.

And he gave me this pitying look, the look that people who've been around a bit give the truly naive, and said, "It *is* Gilbeys. I never order anything else". And I should have left it at that, but you don't when you're young, so I said, "Come off it. Everyone knows Booth's is a yellowy colour, and so is that".

So he waited until the three old girls were rambling on about Donald Peers or some other crooner, and murmured, "Look, I didn't think we were going to get into this, but it's actually 95 per cent Gilbeys Gin and 5 per cent Gilbeys Royal Anchor Brown Sherry. All right?" All right. I grew up a bit that day.

They all talked racing all the time, especially when the jumps started. Of course, this was back in the sensible days when there were separate seasons, and a two-month break in the summer, and occasional freeze-ups when you could back Fontwell at 3'1 to be the first meeting back on. Not like now, when there mustn't be gaps under any circumstances, and much of the fare is cannon-fodder for the shops.

The King George was lost to the weather in 1970, when I was still at the Jockey Club, and dominated by Pendil in the year I sold booze. Wayward Lad won the first two years that I worked with Peter Bromley on BBC Radio, followed by Burrough Hill Lad in 1984.

I remember that year with particular affection, because I drove all the way from my parents-in-law's house in Port Navas, Cornwall, to Kempton, and there was snow on the ground on the A303 and some of the meetings were off, though it was warmer in the London area.

Wayward Lad

It was a great finish that year, with John Francome just getting up to deny Colin Brown on Combs Ditch. The way things work at the BBC, then as now, is that the commentator commentates and then the man who does the prices, in this case me, goes out to record all the interviews for *Sports Report*. (Apart from anything else, this means that the commentator can listen to the piece at home while the interviewer is still stuck in traffic somewhere between Sunbury and Hounslow, but I wouldn't have missed those years with Peter for anything. I really wouldn't....)

Everything went extremely well. Then again, you'd have to be lacking in some way if you failed to get good material out of Francome and Jenny Pitman, who was in splendid form, as I recall. Funnily enough, I left the course with the pair of them and a grumbling David Elsworth, who clearly felt that Combs Ditch should have won, maybe because Colin should have kicked on at some point, though I don't remember the details.

Apart from being a great jockey and a very funny man, there is a genuine kindness about Francome, who explained in some detail that there was very little Colin could have done, and that the best horse had won on the day. Whether David was convinced or not is open to doubt, though his own glory years with Desert Orchid were only just around the corner.

In the end, we gravitate towards people of our own age. When I went to see Elsworth a while back for a magazine piece, he welcomed me with the words, "Ian! It's good to see you. I can't get on with the younger journalists, you know". Thanks very much.

He is an outstanding trainer, but not a man to cross. I remember after one convivial lunch in London, the talk turned to dual-purpose handlers and who was the greatest of the post-war era. With all due respects to the late Captain H Ryan Price, that would be a straight fight between Elsworth and Peter Easterby. Even now, I would not care to choose between them, though you could argue that David had the edge on the Flat, where he won top-class races like the Champion Stakes with In The Groove. Easterby's supporters would no doubt counter with his Gold Cup and Champion Hurdle record.

Desert Orchid was a charismatic steeplechaser and a very gifted one, but getting him to win 'the wrong way round' in bottomless ground at Cheltenham was a master stroke. Elsworth, of course, believed him capable of anything, and there were times when he lost patience with owner Richard Burridge's understandable desire to keep the horse safe at all costs.

Desert Orchid

In the battle of wills, it was a one-all draw overall. Elsworth went very quiet and moody when Burridge considered withdrawing from the 1989 Gold Cup – thank heaven the trainer's implacable nature gained the day – but was never going to persuade the owners to go for the Grand National. I interviewed him a few times then, and have no doubt he thought Desert Orchid would take the National in his stride, wrong way round or no. The starting price, with the nation's money riding on one horse, would certainly have been interesting. Around 5'2 is my guess, but we were never to find out.

Elsworth goes his own way. Touched by genius, an overworked word these days, there is still something of the irascible street-trader about him. "The Arabs came knocking once or twice, but I couldn't get on with them," he told me on one occasion. To which the polite response was: "Really?"

He seems to have worked his way through the odd fortune here and there, and still bounced back without complaint. For that alone one might admire him, though he inspires affection, as well. You're always pleased to see David Elsworth, which is all that matters in the end.

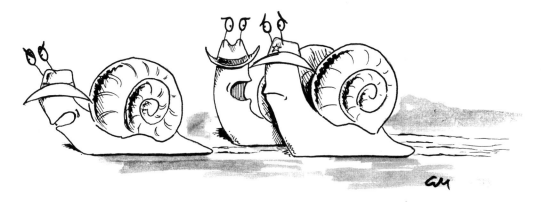

I'm equally fond of his fellow-trainer Jim Old, who sends me the occasional cartoon, though not this one, which I thought I'd pass on anyway. There are these three snails, and two of them are level with each other, while the other one is about an inch and a half in front, and they're all wearing cowboy hats. And one of them turns to his companion and says, "Forget it, sheriff. He's long gone".

How long would it take me to think of something like that? Too long, I reckon.

two

The Carousel Of Time

Archer Street Remembered

It doesn't really matter when you do the work, as long as you do it. I tell myself this is true, listening to the jazz tapes in The Old Duke in mid-afternoon. Not that I know much about jazz, although I saw the Modern Jazz Quartet at Ronnie Scott's many years ago, and Ella Fitzgerald and the Stan Kenton Orchestra.

People had heard all of Ronnie's jokes before, but he had this wonderfully dry way of delivering them. He also managed to keep the club open against all odds. "When I die," he said, "I want to be cremated and have my ashes scattered over my accountant". There were only a couple of dozen people in one night when Blossom Dearie (an acquired taste) was on. It was a bit quiet and Ronnie said, "Right. Let's all join hands and try to contact the living".

Benny Green was determined not to miss a friend's funeral in Golders Green, but he had a very bad back at the time, and the only way he could attend was in a station wagon, propped up on pillows but otherwise flat-out. Even then, he could only just see out of the window. Walking back from the grave, Ronnie spotted him and said, "Hardly worth going home, is it?"

He died a few years ago – gave up the ghost, actually, when a serious gum disorder prevented him from playing the sax – but the club is still there, which is more than you can say for Charlie Chester's casino in Archer Street. As far as I could make out, Charlie had had nothing to do with the place for many years, but the people who ran it kept his name above the door. They had theme nights at Charlie's sometimes, and the croupiers would dress up as cowboys and cowgirls. It was good of them not to shout "Yee-hah!" and slap their thigh when they beat you at blackjack, which was most of the time.

Charlie lived to a good age and was on Radio 2 on Sunday afternoons. He was originally a music hall comedian, though, with a fund of risqué stories, like the one about the man who had a magic mirror on his bathroom door. "Mirror, mirror, on the door: make my manhood touch the floor". And, of course, his legs fell off.

I miss *The Sporting Life*. There was a time when you could buy a copy at 11.30 pm on the corner of Marble Arch and Edgware Road and study the next day's form in the wee small hours. Many years ago Lord Wigg told the magistrate that this had been his firm intention, though his case was weakened slightly by the fact that there aren't many newspaper vendors in mini-skirts calling you "darling".

I used to read the *Life* in Charlie's and then it was a question of getting from Paddington to Reading in time for the 6.20, a quiet, unobtrusive two-carriage affair which, remarkably enough, went all the way to Penzance after Bristol. I wrote quite a few pieces on that train, and even an after-dinner speech on one occasion. As I say, it doesn't matter when you do the work.

Connor The Calvinist

At Cambridge, David Ashforth, Jeff Connor and I spent quite a lot of time in the Jesus Lane betting office. The wallpaper was of the Indian restaurant variety, which made several of the customers feel at home. And there were rude drawings – quite imaginative, some of them. One chap never got a dog forecast up in the three years we were there, but had a rare talent for depicting female ecstasy in its advanced stages. It's sad when people miss their vocation. Anyway, he was warned off when strangers came in to see the drawings without having a bet.

The Jesus Lane shop was run by three characters whom Jeff and I called Foxy, Nice Man and Moonface. Moonface had some sort of problem that could only be soothed by vast quantities of Lucozade. He used to take a huge swig, screw the cap back on, and say, "How can *that* win?' He was in love with the game but appalled by results. Years later I knew a man who was utterly fascinated by one of the working girls in Shepherd Market off Curzon Street. He would even buy her cups of tea at one of the pavement cafes before she put on her harder face and went to work. As a masochist he ran Moonface pretty close, though he had more money and favoured scotch and water over Lucozade.

David and I ended up as racing journalists, one of us a proper one, but Jeff was a chemist. We regret losing touch with him, because he was great company and no mean judge when it came to steeplechases. He was probably the first form student I knew who did not allow a long absence to worry him if he really fancied one.

The Paddy Power Gold Cup was still the Mackeson when Jeff pronounced Jupiter Boy a certainty in 1968, and in those days Fred Rimell was undoubtedly the trainer to follow. Jupiter Boy won quite easily, at a time when Rimell farmed the race, winning with Chatham and Gay Trip (twice) as well.

Jeff followed racing avidly for the first two terms each year, but there was a calvinistic streak in him which led to long days and nights behind locked doors when the exams loomed. He was rewarded with a double first, while those of us cut in half by the wind whistling across the Fens at the Craven Meeting had to settle for a 2:2. Why stay in, reading Tartuffe, when you can go to Newbury and see Willie Carson win on him at 100'6?

Ah Yes, I Remember It Well

Given intelligence and restraint, people who study racing all their life are probably justified in saying they could have made the game pay if the rules had stayed the same. There was a song in the sixties, by Joni Mitchell perhaps, remarking on our fate as "captives on the carousel of time".

> *We can't return, we can only look*
> *Behind from whence we came;*
> *And go round and round*
> *And round, in the circle game.*

It was real late-night stuff. If you played it twice, then Judy Collins' 'Hey, That's No Way To Say Goodbye', and a burst of Leonard Cohen, you were ready to jump without a parachute. Or at least give lectures a miss. But the bit about not returning is accurate enough. In the Jesus Lane shop, you could put four shillings (20p) on at Tote odds, although it was best to wait until Nice Man was free, because Foxy would moan and groan about it and Moonface was on the Lucozade, complaining about the previous result.

The Tote pool never saw the money. It was just a question of the shop offering that particular facility. When each new National Hunt season started I represented a minor threat, because I was alive to all Ron Smyth novice hurdlers and their ability to win first time up. 16'1 on the book was invariably twice that on the machine. All right, you can say that Tote odds are widely available in the High Street now, but back then it was a question of shopping around. When a Ron Smyth hurdler went in first time up, I had this feeling that I was the only person in the country to have backed it on the Tote, away from the course. Years later, when I'd written about him in *The Sporting Life*, Ron sent me a lovely letter, saying he thought I was probably right.

Another thing we can't return to, unfortunately, is the clear separation between Flat and jumps. My late mother always preferred National Hunt racing and would look forward to the new season starting – after a two-month break – in early August. In those days, Dick Francis had a column in the *Sunday Express* with inside information on the early Newton Abbot and Market Rasen meetings. I doubt that she missed any of his winners.

Strangely enough, the whole business about a new season starting and Ron Smyth getting one ready reached its climax when my mother came to live with us several years ago. She had reached that stage of Alzheimer's Syndrome where everything is pure repetition and the desire to be off down the street (not bothering with the pavement) hard to deflect. I was struggling to keep her happy with cups of tea whilst monitoring the first televised Newbury NH meeting.

Since the day in question, I have not worried much about near misses. After all, in a long gambling life there will be short-heads either way and the killer ace the dealer turns to send you back out on to the street, the Reading bench, and the not-so-warm embrace of the 6.20 to Penzance. But I did actually ring Coral's, only to get the engaged tone. And the Ron Smyth hurdler couldn't really win if you looked at his Flat form, which was virtually non-existent, and I was only going to have £20 each-way on him.

What I remember of it now is: my mother still hell-bent on returning to Southampton from Bristol, the kettle working up a head of steam, the second, despairing call to the Barking boys – "I'm afraid they're running there, sir" – an unavailing prayer, and then Sir Peter O'Sullevan's dulcet tones calling this no-hoper home. It wasn't a short head, of course. Ron's horse won easily. He was returned at 25'1 and his name was Problem Child. It took me no more than a year or two to appreciate the irony of that. And I still made the cup of tea, and gazed at my mother as she drank it, realising it was probably best that she couldn't see what a gambler I'd become. Alzheimer's is a terrible thing, but no-one suffering from it worries about old age or death.

Fred West And Other Characters

As the man said, it's strange the way things turn out. I have met quite a few of the people I idolised as a child, including Bill Wightman, who was always my hero. I went to his 90th birthday party last year and he is still hale and hearty, if a little forgetful. Mick Channon trains Digital for him 30 years after Bill gave the former Southampton and England man his first success with Cathy Jane. (Has this ever happened before, outside members of the same family? I suppose so, but not very often.)

Channon later bred Jamesmead from Cathy Jane and one of Wightman's best sprinters, Import. During my years in the wine trade in the 70s I danced up and down in Marylebone High Street as Import just held on in the Wokingham. Imagine that: needing to go out of the office to watch the race through a shop window. How times have changed. Anyway, I watched this desperate finish alongside an Irish gentleman of leisure, who assured me Import had won 'by half a head', so I bought him a can of Carlsberg Special.

The horse was fully entitled to win top handicaps because he was later good enough to finish third in a July Cup – one of only two occasions my wife has ventured inside a betting office. I was away at the time, and she staked £5 each-way at 25'1, keeping the winnings as I recall. But the High Street emporium with its habitual losers left her distinctly unimpressed. I know what she means. As a colleague at SIS used to say, "You never *win* your bollocks, do you? You always lose, or 'do' them". Strange, really.

Albert Martin – Betting Without

I should have backed Chatham as well as Jupiter Boy because he was owned by Charlie Knott, who has a road named after him in

Southampton in the area where he ran the ice hockey, speedway and greyhound stadiums.

Not many people remember greyhound racing in Southampton but it flourished for a while and Alf, later Sir Alf, Ramsey never missed a meeting. By the time I became interested you had to get a coach to Portsmouth, which was the nearest track. There were some fascinating characters there, especially among the bookmakers. There was J Clark of Brighton, who still stands at horserace meetings to this day, although I believe his daughter does much of the work; Fred West, a Southampton layer who never thought his name would be famous; and old Albert Martin.

Albert used to bet 'without'. We all took this to mean without the favourite, although Bill Francis, general manager at Portsmouth since Noah was a lad, once told me he thought Albert was betting without any money. They were great nights, especially when greyhounds came from as far afield as Swindon and Oxford for Open races. And the oxtail soup, scalding hot, was simply, in the modern phrase, to die for. It was just a pity the lady serving it poured half in the paper cup and the other half over your hand. "Mind now, it's piping hot," she used to say, as you jumped up and down.

Park Royal – Another World

I was very fond of greyhound racing and I knew one or two big punters. During my time at Extel some 26 years ago, there was a colleague who thought nothing of having £200 on a favourite at the Hackney BAGS meetings. I must say I struggled to come to grips with that, because the first prize was often about £35. I'm not suggesting there was anything 'iffy' about Hackney, but I do think you need to be careful when your own wager on any event is far bigger than the prize-money. We used to bet in the Mecca shop in Fetter Lane, just up from the White Swan, a legendary watering hole in the great days of Fleet Street but just an ordinary boozer now.

I discovered recently that John McCririck and I were not the only ones who went to Park Royal greyhounds on Monday and Friday afternoons. I interviewed Ricky George, who scored one of the most famous FA Cup goals of all time when Hereford knocked out Newcastle in 1972, and he said he used to go to Park Royal when he was an apprentice at Tottenham. In the great double-winning team of 1961, inside-left Les Allen was the man with all the information, and Ricky was in clover for a while.

You used to get off the tube at Hanger Lane on the North Circular Road, where a coach was waiting to take you to the stadium – a great big old-fashioned place next to the Guinness Brewery. It was sheer escapism, especially on Fridays with the weekend fast approaching. The area itself is a depressing outpost, though it achieved fame of a sort through *Guardian* columnist Jack Trevor Story's novel *I Sit In Hanger Lane*.

He also wrote a trilogy about the fictional tally-boy (hire purchase collector) Albert Argyle, memorably portrayed in the film *Live Now, Pay Later* by Ian Hendry. Story was the sort of novelist we used to read when days were longer and life seemed more innocent. It's hard to resist someone of whom the blurb says, "Jack Trevor Story lives in a caravan in the Hertfordshire woods with a small black poodle".

A Good Man, A Troubled Man

1982 was something of a watershed year for me. I finally joined BBC Radio full-time after doing countless freelance shifts for them, including overnight ones when you prepared the sport scripts for the *Today* programme on Radio 4. The late Brian Redhead used to come on and say, "Good morning, it's Wednesday June the 3rd: Derby Day," which is hard to imagine now, even if they hadn't switched the race to Saturday and guaranteed its anonymity in the welter of summer sport.

I remember the 1982 Hennessy Gold Cup, which was won by Bregawn under a big weight, because I managed to tip him and then interviewed Michael Dickinson afterwards. Making money at gambling is often about identifying something before the world joins in. Thus, Jeff Connor was a great Tony Dickinson man when he held the licence, happy to accept short prices in novice chases because the horses were so immaculately schooled. Michael continued the tradition and I have no doubt he was,

Bregawn

and is, a brilliant trainer. But he nursed plenty of self-doubt, and each major triumph was greeted with a bizarre mixture of joy and overwhelming relief.

He was as helpful to the media as anyone I have ever known – on a par say, with Trevor Brooking, Josh Gifford and Clive Brittain. When he saddled the first five in the Cheltenham Gold Cup, I'd asked Michael where he would watch the race from and whether I could have the first interview for Radio 2 afterwards. He said this would be no problem.

He watched events unfold on television in the sponsors' room next door to the weighing-room. Not surprisingly, he was in quite a state as the five of them followed each other up the hill. I would have bet quite a lot of money that the interview would be shuffled down the batting order, and the last thing a radio man wants to see at such a time is a television camera, complete with ever-genial host, appearing round the corner. But Dickinson stopped, did the piece live to Radio 2 before anything else, and *asked if it was all right*. I said I felt sure it was.

Some months later, I asked him if he remembered the piece. "Remember it?" he said. "I've got a copy of the tape. I play it in the car whenever I feel depressed about things". I never really knew why he felt depressed about anything, or why the job with

Robert Sangster didn't work out (though I have an idea), but I realised at that moment that he would always be driving himself on, proving things to himself over and over again. It was a good decision to go to America because he'd have had no peace at all here.

Round And Round…

I drove back across Cambridge the other day. The Jesus Lane shop has been gone for many years, and the last time I saw Moonface he was leaning on the rails at the July course, shaking his head in disbelief. There was a bulge in his inside pocket, and I knew what that was, although it would have been interesting to know which flavour he preferred.

The Marsh pub down by the docks in Southampton is all boarded up, which is a pity because it was a good place for 'morning after' analysis. And I'd have to be honest and say Portsmouth greyhound stadium is not quite what it was during the great Bill Francis days. There used to be a vast, twinkling Tote board at one end, but now it's a used car lot. Even The Dell has gone the way of Park Royal. I think it was Andy Sipowitz in *NYPD Blue* who said that regret for the past is a waste of human spirit, but it's hard to avoid sometimes.

We can't return, we can only look behind from whence we came. And even then, Proust says we only remember the places so clearly because we know what we were thinking at the time.

"The places we have known do not belong only to the world of space on which we map them for our own convenience. The memory of a particular image is but regret for a particular moment. And houses, roads, avenues are as fugitive, alas, as the years."

So there you are. And you thought you'd be getting some help with your Ten To Follow.

three

Discreet Enquiries – Short Story, 1990

Lennie sounds guarded, of course. Not respectful, just guarded. "Isn't this rather an unusual call?" he asks. "I'm a jockey, not a trainer. It's Hopgood you want, surely?"

"Hopgood said she'd win last time," I reply coolly. "That was before she found more blind alleyways than anyone knew existed at Folkestone and came fifth." I try to keep the bitterness out of my voice.

He chuckles softly. It's a dry, Liverpool sound, timeless in its knowledge of human weakness. "Well, I didn't ride her that day," he says. "You'd have to ask good old Arnie. He's ridden for Hopgood since time began. I wouldn't talk to him on the phone though. These days you never know who's listening, do you?" The laugh takes on a harder edge.

He has me pretty well worked out and I haven't even come to the point. A deep breath. "Look, she's a syndicate horse," I begin. "Quite a few people in the group don't know that much about the game and it's a real letdown when she runs much worse than Hopgood says she will. All I'm asking is what you think about tomorrow."

I'm ashamed to feel my heart thumping insistently against my shirt. I wish I'd never rung him. That's the difference between three drinks and four.

He's too hard to let me get away with it. "Listen Mr. B, don't break my heart. Those people you've brought together are too flush to worry about the odd disappointment. They don't back horses for real, so it's you we're talking about, isn't it?"

It's pointless to argue, and he takes my hesitation to mean he's got it right. I wonder in passing how he views owners who normally command respect. I'm relieved that I let him go on, though.

"I rode that filly at Yarmouth, and if she can't win a poxy Brighton seller there's something wrong. I'll be trying, if that's what you're worried about, and neither Hopgood nor anyone else can change that. I can't afford to have my collar felt again, and I don't need calls like this."

He holds on just long enough for me to mutter thanks. He has no need to adhere to the usual jockey-owner relationship, and we both know I won't be contacting him again.

———————

I get through the morning. Part of it is spent making sure the betting arrangements are in hand. I don't bother much with the racing papers because the last thing you need at this stage is a couple of stars by her name, but in fact she's not widely tipped. I walk all the way along the front towards Hove and, as so often in the past, promise myself an identical journey 24 hours later, to compare moods.

Eleven o'clock isn't too early to arrive at The Grand. Vodka in heavy glasses and money everywhere. The members of the syndicate make their appearance soon afterwards. Nothing changes in the conversation. House prices are serious, the latest news from the City is all-important and school fees are scandalous, but horseracing is a game and this is a day out.

"But let's ask Mr. B. He's the expert, after all, and he fancied her last time, isn't that right, Mr. B?" In a perverse way they love you to be wrong. It probably strengthens their belief that they're not missing anything by staying at arm's length.

I smile winningly and make encouraging noises. I'm good with the blue rinses and check jackets. They know I know the game.

The atmosphere is much the same at the track. Hopgood comes on with that dreadful false bonhomie, flattering the women and joshing the men, but things go quiet five minutes before she's due to canter down.

Lennie arrives barely in time to offer a single pleasantry and says nothing to Hopgood, thus confirming the long-held belief that most meaningful trainer-jockey conversations take place a long way from the parade ring and conveniently by-pass the owner.

It's not difficult to oversee the syndicate's investments yet still watch the race alone. I go high up in the old-fashioned stand and try to let my mind go blank. My legs ache, there's a dull throbbing in my chest, and the first trickle from the armpits makes it descent.

I look across the housing estate; thousands of people living mundane lives, united principally by their complete indifference to the petty drama being played out above them. Not for the first time, this particular October meeting feels like the October of life.

How do I describe the ride he gives her? Indolent comes closest, I suppose, indolent and slightly cruel. In a field of 12 he ambles along at the back for half of the mile journey. He pushes her through a gap where you have to on the final bend, but doesn't send her on until they reach those caravans at the furlong-pole. She's going to win anyway but he hits her once, twice, to make absolutely sure. He's a tough little bastard.

And I'm shouting, of course I am, shouting and yelling until the sound of my own relief threatens to shatter the eardrums. Because when genuine excitement is dead, there's only relief and despair left. Today relief has it. Pathetic to you, maybe, but lifeblood to me.

Hopgood accepts his share of backslapping and cheek-kissing and looks me in the eye for the first time. "9'2 to 11'4, they tell me," he murmurs. "Well, well. Someone must think I know what I'm doing after all."

"Do we buy her in?" He makes quite sure no-one else can hear. "I really don't care a twopenny damn what you do," he replies.

"You're the sportsman, you decide," and turns away without another word.

―――――――

You want it to be perfect, but it never is. We get her back cheaply and the champagne flows, but it's difficult to feel part of it now. Hopgood's words leave a nasty taste and I need to be on my own – a quiet restaurant, a little self-indulgence and the usual calculations.

Even so, I stay until the end and Lennie rides the last winner as well. It's a 25'1 shot, and maybe he stays for a little celebration himself, because the car park is almost deserted when I see him hurrying away from Members.

I have the instinctive feeling he'd walk a brisk half-mile to avoid conversation, but he passes so close that it's impossible. I startle him but he recovers and nods curtly.

"Thanks for today," I say.

He shrugs, and that hard glitter comes into his eyes. "Quite a day, Mr. B. You and Hopgood both have it away and neither of you knows what the other one's up to. The boys had a bit of a laugh about that." His mouth turns down in a mirthless grin.

"I don't think I can have horses with him any more. He knows I rang you, doesn't he?"

"So what? He's in no position to complain. He phoned immediately afterwards as a matter of fact, just to let me know how much he fancied her. If it makes you feel any better, you were dead right about Folkestone. I asked around and some of the lads were amazed Arnie wasn't pulled in. Still, win some, lose some."

I feel that tide of weariness which embraces all gamblers sooner or later. "It doesn't make me feel any better," I say.

"Yeah, well, that's up to you. It's none of my business and I don't want it to be, but there's one big difference between you and Hopgood. He'll make today count for a good long time, but you'll need another cute little set-up in a couple of weeks. Just remember, I'm not on your list of contacts."

He's about half my age and moves away quickly to where his BMW is parked near the exit. I watch him all the way, and catch the fragment of some current tune carried back on the breeze. He wears his loneliness well.

There's a definite chill in the air now and the lights are shimmering through a hint of sea-fret on the front. I turn up my collar and set off down the hill.

four

Farewell To Old Friends

You may safely assume that any recommendations from this quarter have involved plenty of midnight oil, a bit of George Shearing in the background, someone I can't identify singing 'How Insensitive', and not too much Pinot Grigio. The fact is, I need winners even more than you do.

Not so long ago a weekly magazine I wrote for went under, the Venice restaurant in Great Titchfield Street closed and a middle-aged lady, getting a rare tune out of a Vauxhall Frontera, came roaring up over the hill and drove straight into my garage.

I'd have put it down to passion, except that the doors weren't open. *'Jamais deux sans trois'*, as the French say, when things start to go wrong. All of this and Adam Faith gone, too. It should be *'Jamais trois sans quatre'*. Can't trust them to get anything right.

I cannot quite come to terms with the closure of the Venice, an Italian restaurant I have frequented since 1979. The memories tumble over each other. I have written many pieces in there, struggled with deadlines, given up a job after a couple of glasses too many, placed a £2,000 bet which won, dozed in the doorway waiting for the sun to come up, filmed a video to launch Ladbrokes Sporting Spreads, met Neil Kinnock and watched Trevor McDonald wander up and down as though being a personality meant nothing to him at all. Which is what they all do, of course, and we don't really mind, except when they think we can't see through it.

The Venice was also the venue for *The Sporting Life's* farewell party in May, 1998. It cost me quite a lot at the time – the loss of work, not the party – although, as a freelance, you get used to these things. *The Life* had been going for 137 years and some people thought it would last forever, but nothing does.

Like a good many of my racing contemporaries, I grew up with the paper. It was in my inside pocket at school – Doubtful Character winning at 20'1 at Carlisle is an early, happy memory – and the Lincoln Handicap plans were up on the wall in my room at Cambridge at least a month before the race took place. I think Tom Jones' Waterloo Place was the closest I ever came to finding the winner, a task which became no easier with the passing of the years. I made Chukaroo a certainty when they ran it on the round course, but he was struck into on the bend and virtually pulled up.

In these days when racing politics, not to mention the whiff of corruption, dominate the front pages, buying the *Life* and finding out what Augur thought would win the 3.45 at Pontefract seems part of a different lifetime. The paper covered all the stories, of course, but everyone knew that Friday was the big day for political comment because that was when Jack Logan's column appeared.

Logan – Sir David Llewellyn – was a campaigning journalist who kept beating the drum until the powers that be picked up the rhythm. That was how crash helmets on the gallops became compulsory, and the racing world is in his debt. He delighted some readers and infuriated others, with the result that the letters' page was sometimes the most entertaining thing in the paper. Perhaps we all view the past through rose-tinted glasses, but it would be a particularly easy-going man who failed to find the welter of comment, opinion and reaction these days excessive. It just washes over you in the end. We are not 'rocked' or 'shaken' by anything that happens, and we have been around long enough to know that "our switchboard was jammed" means a couple of people rang up. So it goes on.

Regrettably, unlike Logan I have never orchestrated a campaign designed to save lives, but there are one or two things I'd do away with at a stroke. In particular, the glowing compliments to tipping services where only the writer's initials are published.

"Dear Sirs, Just a line to say a big thank-you for the wonderful run of results recently. I have tried many other services, but yours is truly the best." A.K., Barnstaple.

"Dear Sirs, I took your promises with a pinch of salt" (why did you subscribe then, you wally) "but the target has been reached inside three months, not twelve! Keep up the good work!" R.T., Solihull.

"Dear Sir or Madam, I thought your results on the Flat took some beating, but over the jumps you really are the business. Already I have paid for a new garage" (can I have the old one?) "and the wife and I are off to Ibiza next week. First class, of course. Just like your service!" (Stone me.) P.W., Aberystwyth.

It's all harmless enough, although you'd need to wear one of those funny coats which do up at the back to take any of it seriously. I just wish some of the offerings were a bit more imaginative.

"Hola hombres! Here I am on the beach at Marea de Portillo. Si! In Cuba! Sipping my third daiquiri and puffing on a Havana. Olive-skinned senoritas at my beck and call, and all thanks to your sensational tipping. Es fantastico, eh? Back in time for Fakenham on Monday. Gracias, amigos. Keep up the good work!" K.T., Penge.

No, I wouldn't believe that one either, especially the Penge bit, but I quite like it.

Anyway, must close now with a Folkestone seller to solve. It's a very sad song, 'How Insensitive'. "What can you say, when a love affair is over?" Search me, chief. I can't even work out who the vocalist is. It's not Astrud Gilberto, Dinah Washington or Julie London, though. It's some other person.

five

Low Life, High Old Times

Jeffrey Bernard and Bob, who works in a Bristol post office, have one thing in common: they are both ahead on my tips. Bob even sent me a Christmas card, having backed Quito right through the 2003 Flat. Sadly, Jeffrey has departed for a better place – "gone on ahead," as the Australians say – a rather drastic way of making sure he stayed in front.

I did not know him well, though we spent a lost afternoon at Goodwood in the eighties and something won at 9'2. Jeffrey had made a mental note of it before the vodka session began and was very impressed. The bar actually ran out of his preferred tipple before close of play, so I think we need say no more.

I learned from him that there is no point in trying to write for everyone. In a way, *The Spectator*, a bastion of old Conservatism, was an odd place to find his celebrated Low Life column. Memorably described as "a weekly suicide note", it must have baffled the magazine's crustier devotees whilst delighting students in WH Smith who devoured it without the slightest intention of buying a copy.

Bernard adored racing and his *Sporting Life* column was arguably the funniest thing ever to appear in the paper. He lost the job eventually, of course, having disgraced himself at a point-to-point dinner, but the *Life* was the loser and Lord Oaksey once opined that it was mad not to have him back.

He behaved appallingly at times, but did the sort of things that others can only dream about. Like the time he stood by a Rolls Royce at Stratford races and pretended to be a beggar. It was only an April Fools' Day prank, but one old lady pressed 25p into his hand and said: "You poor man. It must be terribly hard to run a car like that".

On 2000 Guineas' day he filed the same column five times during the afternoon, and at Tattersalls Yearling Sales he once bid a hundred guineas for a horse, only to forget all about it until Henry Cecil reminded him the next day. Former trainer Doug Marks – quite a character himself – apologised to Tattersalls on his behalf and asked them to take the horse back, Bernard's bank account containing the princely sum of eleven shillings (55p) at the time.

But he was funny, and he could write when he put his mind to it, making much of today's output appear formulaic by comparison. Towards the end of his tenure at the *Life*, he spent some time on the early-morning gallops, "ghost-like columns coming out of the mist, stirrups and bits jangling, horses snorting. As they peeled in twos and galloped off, the slamming of hooves into damp turf produced that intoxicating rhythm which somehow always makes the hair stand up on the back of your neck and the pulse beat a little faster".

When Keith Waterhouse wrote the play *Jeffrey Bernard Is Unwell,* in which the eponymous hero spends a night locked in Soho's Coach and Horses pub and reflects on his life, Peter O'Toole was the perfect choice to play the lead. That could not be said of either James Bolam or Tom Conti, who followed. Bolam, a racing man, carried it off reasonably well but has always been difficult or downright prickly with the press, while Conti certainly did not approve of Bernard. As Jeff once said to him, "How can you play me if you don't like me?"

But O'Toole and Bernard might almost have been blood brothers. O'Toole's father styled himself 'Captain Pat', although his only captaincy had been that of a minor professional football team. As the actor tells us in *Loitering With Intent,* the first part of his autobiography, "Captain Pat lived his thirties and early fortiess as an itinerant, racetrack bookmaker. Poker was known, as were chemmy shoes, spinning wheels, balls of all sorts, dicing, horse-racing. Yes, he would, when the bag was healthy, step off the stool, loan possession of it to his associate, Red Dan the tic-tac man, depart the Silver Ring and go punting in Tatts."

That Bernard always let tomorrow take care of itself is not in doubt, while O'Toole has freewheeled through life, the bohemian sometimes acknowledging the ambitious thespian. "Our treasury at that time, when we (the painter O'Liver and I) were both aged twenty, had held a couple of quid apiece and a crisp fiver that I had recently extorted from a loving relative. This we had happily blown on beer, pork pies, whisky and good seats at Guys and Dolls."

O'Toole considered Sam Levene's playing of Nathan Detroit one of the great performances of the age. But what comes across even more clearly is that particular West End production's faithfulness to the book – "a glorious hymn to Runyon" – as O'Toole puts it. "O'Liver and I, softly howling to each other snippets of the words and melodies, had swayed back to our residence in leafy Green Park and had thought not of tomorrow, our priority being getting through another night."

Not the sort of thing to appeal to a buttoned-up *Daily Mail* reader, perhaps. But Jeffrey Bernard would have loved it.

Kicking Bird's Revenge

Apparently there is to be a new version of *The Sound Of Music* with a different ending. After a rousing chorus of 'Edelweiss', the von Trapps try to make it to the border but are intercepted by the Lonely Goatherd, who guns them down. Been lonely too long, see. Too much time on his own, thinking about things. Tone deaf, as well.

All right, I made it up. But there are some good stories to come out of *The Sound Of Music*, referred to by Christopher Plummer as "the sound of mucous". Jane Leevis, who plays Daphne in *Frasier*, says she always used to think that Peggy Wood, who plays the Mother Superior, had come out with a very rude line. "What is it about the abbey you can't face, Maria?" Something about the way Peggy pronounces the word "can't," I believe.

I don't know why I thought of it, really, except that I was watching *My Fair Lady* over Christmas and thinking how unlucky Julie Andrews had been to miss out as Eliza Doolittle, and how well she coped with the disappointment. There's nothing wrong with Audrey Hepburn's performance – well, not too much anyway – and Hollywood obviously needed her name to guarantee box-office receipts world-wide, but Andrews was perfect on stage and would have been just as good in the film.

At least Wilfrid Hyde-White was ideally cast as Rex Harrison's friend and confidant. An inveterate gambler, Wilfrid once appeared at the bankruptcy courts in Carey Street and was asked by the bench why someone in his parlous position was staying at the Savoy Hotel. "Well, I believe you'll be seeing quite a lot of me and it's only just around the corner," he said.

I sometimes watch films in the mornings now, when I'm not studying Class H Banded races at Wolverhampton. I'm fond of Class G sellers and even sponsor one at Brighton, but I must say I never expected to see six races like that on the same card. Still, that's progress for you.

I'm working steadily through Marcel Proust and trying to model myself on the boulevardier and Jockey Club member Swann, which is not particularly easy in Nailsea. By the way, I came across a curious fact the other day. There are no casinos in the big French cities, they're all on the coast or in spa towns like Enghien. So you can get cleaned out and cleaned in at the same time.

In America, most of the casinos are on Indian reservations, thus proving that revenge is a dish best served cold. The Kiowa are involved, having more scores to settle than most. In John Huston's 1959 film *The Unforgiven* they are portrayed as "thieving, murdering devils," and none too bright either, since they continue to circle the ranch where Burt Lancaster and Audie Murphy, determined to hold on to Audrey H, their foundling 'sister', even though she is of Kiowa blood, pick them off one by one. Setting fire to the place would have been the logical move, of course, but the film would have been shorter and the ending rather different.

Hollywood is more politically correct these days, and would find a way of acknowledging that the Kiowa were very harshly treated. They were prevented from hunting buffalo and forced to plant corn instead, but even then the wily chief Kicking Bird, who was part Crow, counselled staying on the reservation. When the young braves forced him to act, Kicking Bird, no mean strategist, routed a division of soldiers from Fort Richardson, Texas (so it's hard to believe he wouldn't have seen off Burt and Audie), before returning to the reservation and working steadily for peace.

But he couldn't win, the military authorities eventually forcing him to send 26 Kiowa for exile to the dungeons of Fort Marion, Florida. This cost him the respect of his own people, one of whom may even have poisoned him.

His descendants may possibly have noted, with no little irony, that the reservation, hopelessly inadequate for hunting buffalo, offers easily enough space for the construction of casinos and subsequent fleecing of punters, most of them in thrall to the relentless clatter of fruit machines. All in all, it's probably just as well Kicking Bird isn't still around.

The Great And The Good

Gamblers have always fascinated me. The way they talk, the way they celebrate, the way they recover. True gamblers – those to whom the stakes actually make a difference to the way they live – embrace a twilight world both comforting and dangerous.

The most unlikely people have been high rollers, sometimes using the racetrack or the casino as an escape from the outside world. The legendary QC George Carman would play the blackjack tables until 4 am, then go home and prepare himself for an important case, sometimes making do with an hour's sleep or none at all. And this was the man who represented Jeremy Thorpe, Ken Dodd, George Best and countless other household names.

Carman was hardly born with a silver spoon. He worked his way up through Chambers in Manchester and his early casino gambling took place in Salford, not Mayfair. His son Dominic, author of a superb biography, recalls that he would often cash fees from a big case, go straight to the Salford casino and lose the lot.

Dominic and his mother Celia would be obliged to hide when the milkman called for payment.

But Carman lived for the extraordinary buzz that successful gambling can provide. "After a good evening at the tables, he would be visibly energised. It was the same adrenalin rush that he experienced in court. Winnings had to be cash only. That way the bank would never know."

Fascinatingly, in the 'cash for questions' Hamilton v Al-Fayed case, he was able to comment on "how surprisingly slim these bundles are". George knew all about it, of course, because winning nights at the casino brought bundles of £50 notes in plastic wallets containing £2,500 in all. The piles of cash were kept in an unlocked sideboard drawer at Evelyn Gardens in Chelsea, before making their way back to Curzon Street and the casinos. When I played blackjack many years ago a friend always had a pile of £5 chips by the bed, thus guaranteeing that, no matter how badly things turned out on any given night, there was always the chance he might hit back with his 'reserves' some stray afternoon.

I try to avoid far-fetched stories, but there is no doubt Walter Matthau made at least two films to pay off his gambling debts, while director Robert Altman (*M*A*S*H, Gosford Park*) headed for the blackjack tables one afternoon, hell-bent on an end it or mend it session after telling his secretary he was not to be disturbed under any circumstances.

Midway through another dreadful run of cards, he was suddenly aware of her presence at his side. "What is it, Helen? I'm losing $30,000 and I thought I told you I was unavailable," he said.

"I'm sorry, Mr Altman," she said, "But your bookie is on the phone".

In the midst of his despair, a true gambler would see the funny side of that.

Feeling No Pain

Italian restaurants, single malts and a self-destructive streak have set me back a bit but I remain reasonably cheerful, despite my facial expression. It's hard to be down for very long when you know another Class H Banded Stakes (Division II) is just around the corner.

People sometimes ask how I started writing, but they never enquire about the first bets. My favourite horses are from years and years ago, and steam radio plays a prominent part. I remember Thames Trader winning at Ally Pally all the time, and an evening when three V's – Vigorik, Vanadium and Vanity Case – all turned up at Wolverhampton.

Who knows why certain things stay in the memory? The Lester Piggott/Scobie Breasley championship race; my dad telling me about Bill Wightman; R.C. Sturdy and Ryan Price entering two and winning with the 'wrong' one, i.e. the right one; Vakil-ul-Mulk at Wincanton; Dougie Marks' Bunto with his great big feet and funny ears; Candid Picture, formerly with Les Hall, winning at 20'1 for Basil Foster at Stockton; interviewing Page 3 girl Linda Lusardi at Sandown and asking whether people ever got tired of them; Limelight going in at Chepstow.

And the first real setback, since you ask, was Peter Easterby's Pablond at a Leicester evening meeting towards the end of the sixties. He was favourite and ran miserably, and I knew, driving back to Cambridge, that no matter what anyone said, there would always be days like that for the simple reason that a horse can't tell you when he doesn't feel like it.

So, the gambler either handles it or he doesn't. And I think back to O'Toole in *Lawrence of Arabia*, holding a naked flame to his arm without flinching. Harry Fowler is impressed and tries it himself, only to drop the match as he cries out in pain.

"Blimey, it hurts!" he says. "What's the trick?"

And O'Toole looks at him soberly and says, "The trick is, *not minding* that it hurts".

six

Stevie And Me – Short Story, 2001

I'll tell it as plainly as I can. I've known Stevie since we were kids at school, running a sweepstakes on the Wokingham and a little game of pontoon on the side.

He never questioned anything. If he liked you, he trusted you. And he had this way of looking you straight in the eye when you were telling him something. "Blimey. I never knew that," he'd say, shaking his head in wonderment.

I can still hear Nobby Clarke, the careers master, saying, "I believe you'll make a success of things, McCall. But look after your friend Stephen Mayes. He's not as sharp as you are."

Sharp. That's a laugh. This morning I was looking for my cleanest dirty shirt before going for an interview. I've run a few pubs and clubs in my time and built them up from nothing. My wife got tired of it, like they do, but we're still friends, sort of.

I told her she should have married an accountant, and she didn't disagree, even when I pointed out that accountants couldn't listen to Miles Davis and Ornette Coleman at ten in the morning. Lizzie was never a jazz fan.

I suppose Nobby was right about Stevie. I remember we were at Portsmouth dogs one night and stopped for a pint of mild in the Harbour Lights on the way home. "You know the song Harbour Lights?" I said. "You'd think they named the pub after it, wouldn't you? But the composer was on a boating holiday and happened to drop anchor close by. When the pub sign lit up it inspired him and he sat down and wrote the song."

Stevie stared at me. "Blimey. That's amazing. How come you know things like that?" he said.

It's hard to say. I don't know why things stay with me, but they're not worth any money, and that's a fact. This was something Olive pointed out when she started going out with Stevie and fell in love with him. Olive quite likes me, I think, but doesn't let it show. It's a game we play.

When they got married we still went to Portsmouth dogs once a week. It was a great place, with some odd characters. The bookie Albert Martin was my favourite. His board said "Betting Without," which meant without the favourite, of course. Stevie watched his every move, often backing the five dog when it was certain to miss the mud on the bends and Albert had scrubbed out one of the railers.

I'd dropped out of law school and was playing sax three nights a week in the Silhouette Club. Stevie was a fitter in the dockyard, but they were laying people off left, right and centre. Olive, as pale and worried-looking as ever, was pregnant with their first child.

We were both quite vulnerable the night it all changed about 15 years ago. It rained hard and I was full of cold. To be honest, if Broken China hadn't been running in the seventh I might even have gone home early, but I'd been waiting for him and you know the way it is.

Albert rubbed out the one dog, which Stevie said would struggle anyway. The five was guaranteed a solo, with Broken China in trap three coming late to catch him, or so we thought.

They were second and third favourites, and we put everything on a reversed forecast. Stevie never did forecasts as a rule and looked tense as they were boxed up. I should have known something was troubling him.

Gambling hard-luck stories are ten a penny, so let's just say we were right but didn't get paid. The five flew out and stayed wide; Broken China, a crafty greyhound but an unlucky one, checked behind the others and nipped between them at the third bend.

He would have picked up the leader in plenty of time but, for the first and only time in his career, the five veered left and hit him so hard that Broken China nearly went over the inside rail. They were so far clear that five still held on from one. Normally, Stevie would have made a small profit. He shrugged and thrust his hands deep inside his pockets. "I was laid off today," he said.

There was a casino at Portsmouth Stadium in those days. I knew the manager and he'd slip us a scotch on the slate after a losing night. You saw some well-heeled punters in there, roulette players mostly, but when the smoothie joined us at the bar I knew he'd followed us in. "No luck?"

Stevie told him the story. I love Stevie, but he has this way of treating total strangers like blood brothers.

"Too bad. Broken China, broken hock. He's been put down, apparently. And how is Mr. McCall? It's Maurice by the way. Maurice Fells."

He was about 40, trying to look 32, and making a fair job of it. His suit wouldn't have left much change out of £600 and his shirt was hand-made. I thought he might be half Arab. He shook hands and said, "That's a mean saxophone you play. The Silhouette Club, I think?"

I knew it was a set-up from then on, but you don't always care, do you? I was cold and tired, and vaguely worried about being skint again. "You must know Southampton as well as you know Portsmouth," I said.

"Oh, I know all the ports. It's my business. Does the Silhouette pay well?"

No, of course it bloody doesn't, but I'm not telling you that, I thought. "What is your business then?" I said.

He looked at me with what Lizzie would have called 'come to bed' eyes, checked that no one else was listening and said, "I find people for certain jobs. I'm well paid for it, and I don't make mistakes. I've watched you for a while, Mr. McCall".

"This is where I ask what I have to do, isn't it?"

"If you like, yes. I want you to take a Mercedes from Portsmouth to St. Malo, and then down to a little place called Martigues, near Marseilles. Someone will meet you there. It's quite warm at this time of year, you know."

Or even hot, I thought. "Of course, I don't ask what's in the Mercedes," I said.

"Don't be over-dramatic. There's just you and the car," Maurice Fells said. "It's £10,000 cash in hand before the first trip, and another £10,000 after the third and final one. Three trips in six weeks. There is no risk. You can fly back if you want to and I pay. After that, we never see each other again. Unlike you, I am not overly fond of greyhound racing, Mr. McCall".

And I'll tell you now, for a minute or two I thought about it. Twenty grand would have been the down payment on a jazz club of my own. A little place in Southsea, with late supper for the right sort of customers.

But I was chilled to the bone, and the Broken China incident had got to me in a way I can't quite explain. So I looked at him and said no, and he smiled and said it was all right and glanced across at Stevie.

And Stevie, his big, uncomplicated face taking in every word, was being chatted up by a brunette at the bar. I could have told her she was wasting her time, because Olive was a distance clear, but I really didn't feel too good, and in any case I could see that Fells was waiting to get a word in.

It's funny, the way things work out. I gave up the dogs for a while and lived quietly but then one night Olive, who was getting near her time, rang me at the Silhouette and asked where the hell Stevie was. I didn't know but afterwards I went round there and held her hand and made all the right noises.

I played the sympathetic best friend rather well, but she was crying and said he kept disappearing, telling her not to worry, which was a bit like telling her not to breathe.

Well, to my great shame I failed to put two and two together, but then again I know Stevie better than you do, and you can take it from me that a trip to France was 50'1 at least. Anyway I went everywhere but couldn't find him, though apparently he turned up just before the baby arrived.

He brought them both into the club while we were rehearsing some Stan Getz material. To be honest, I think he'd had a couple at lunchtime because he kept putting his arm around me and saying I was the best friend a man could ever have, and all the rest of it. Even Olive smiled at me, and I wished I'd brought my camera.

"Between you and me," Stevie said, his voice booming out over Southampton Docks, "that Arab bloke with the English name we met at Pompey dogs was bloody good news. I only ever saw him twice and picked up twenty grand. Nice motor, too. Me and Olive are opening a hardware store in Gosport. What do you think?"

I thought it was great. I've no idea how he found St Malo, never mind Martigues, but I still thought it was great. Now there are Stevie Mayes hardware stores all over Hampshire and Olive has a beauty salon in Fareham. "He's done well, my Stevie, hasn't he?" she says.

Oh, yes indeed. As for me, I struggle on. It's nearly Christmas, and they race at Portsmouth tonight. I think I may have a cold coming on, though.

seven

Buying A Fortune In The Duke

The Old Duke in Bristol is a famous jazz pub. It went through a bad patch when the brewery thought that so many enthusiasts in one place at one time were bound to spend money if offered exotic things, like food. Happily, this basic error having been acknowledged, the Duke is on the way back. Whether it can pay musicians from the beer takings is not something we need worry about here.

Lately I have been dropping in at 11.30 in the morning. It's not every pub which plays a brassy yet mournful version of 'Once Upon a Summertime' when you're trying to come to grips with a tricky handicap hurdle, the Folkestone seller or your life so far.

I have 'Once Upon a Summertime' at home, of course, on an Astrud Gilberto LP. My wife was going to get me a new needle for my 40th birthday, but that was a long, long time ago so it doesn't sound too good. Some people would say it doesn't matter, because Astrud sings pretty flat (which is true) but I happen to like her.

The Old Duke has been kind to me, and I suppose it will take a while yet for the bookmakers to recover the Record Time winnings. Record Time is only moderate, but Eric Alston sent her down to Newmarket for a five-furlong sprint in the summer, and she seemed to have the best of the draw.

It's quiet in the Duke when the lunchtime crowd has gone, so you can ring up your bet, chat amiably to the man at Surrey Racing ("What makes you fancy that one, Mr. Carnaby? What's it got going for it, sir?"); listen to the commentary and the Tote returns – £25.60 in this case, not bad 30 times – and still hear the last few bars of 'I Can't Get Started'.

This week I found myself doodling on a beer mat, working out the combination employed by David Conolly-Smith and his friends in Munich when they landed the near £1m Tote Scoop6. It was $10 \times 8 \times 3 \times 3 \times 3 \times 1$, and my only observation is that I might have come pretty close, too, if someone had let me have 2,160 goes. And I say this as a man who becomes dazed and confused if proven correct more than once every 24 hours.

Reading through his background, I realised that Conolly-Smith, journalist and bookshop owner these days, must have been making the regular trip from Cambridge to Newmarket only a couple of years ahead of me. Maybe his head was full of combination bets even then, whereas I was praying for a miracle payout on one race. It even happened one day, when Peter Walwyn, still on the way up, won a multi-runner maiden (do they have any other sort at Newmarket?) with Creek Alley. The new electronic number board had been installed, and we waited an age to discover that she had paid £36.17.6d for four shillings, or 20p to you. Which is roughly 180'1 for a 20'1 chance on the book.

Whilst this was enough to treat a Cherry Hinton girl in the Turk's Head, it was hardly life changing and nor has anything been since. Thirty-odd years later, pondering a little snifter of Glenmorangie to help the Courage Best on its way, I can see that syndicates are probably the answer where the big pools are concerned.

And yet, and yet. Did you realise that, even when an obliging Munich bookie put up half the stake, Conolly-Smith and his five friends still had to find £400 each? You say it quickly and it all seems perfectly feasible, but I wonder how many of us have five friends like that? We might find five strangers, interested in a business proposition, but who would pick the horses?

Conolly-Smith's real achievement is to have around him a group of people of a certain age, successful in their own right, all prepared to play for quite high stakes and leave the decision making to two experts. And I dare say they'd have shrugged off defeat quite quickly, and started planning again.

I wonder how long it would take to build up the right sort of contacts if I opened a bookshop around the corner from The Old Duke and started coming in at lunchtimes instead of early morning and mid-afternoon? Rather too long, perhaps.
Still, being too late for things brings on a certain relief. I may have that Glenmorangie now.

eight

Four Gamblers

I mention elsewhere that a magazine I wrote for closed down in 2003. This was *The Sports Adviser,* which was highly regarded, I think, but failed to establish itself on a subscription only basis.

Timing was a big problem. These days, betting is so sophisticated that up-to-the-minute information is essential. Therefore, a magazine which went to press on Tuesday evening was never going to satisfy committed weekend gamblers, no matter how much they may have enjoyed the High Roller/Low Roller section on the back page, where Julian Wilson and Mark 'Couch' Winstanley engaged in some highly amusing banter.

I interviewed well over 100 gamblers in just under three years, and might just as easily have chosen four different ones in the section that follows. But I am fond of them because they show how gambling can sometimes be a force for good.

Would Duncan Heath have become chairman of International Creative Management without Charlie Potheen's victory in the 1972 Hennessy Gold Cup? Probably, but we can't be sure. Would Al Alvarez have survived a period of black despair without the comfort of the poker table? Borderline, I'd say.

Anyway, I can tell you that all four are outstanding company, and at least three have recovered from setbacks, financial or emotional, which would have crushed lesser men. Long may they flourish.

Booth Is Back On Track

There are those who will never accept it, but Tony Booth has mellowed. These days, the original "randy Scouse git" of Johnny Speight's seminal sixties series *Till Death Us Do Part* lives quietly in Ireland with his charming wife Steph, working on an idea for a new musical.

For someone who came within a short-head of writing himself off altogether, he looks surprisingly well. As Cherie Blair's father and the man who loved and married Pat Phoenix – Elsie Tanner of Coronation Street – as she lay on her deathbed, he would always have been of considerable interest to the tabloids. In fact, he gave them plenty of material off his own bat. The worst episode came when he suffered near 50 per cent burns in a domestic fire. He was pronounced dead three times in hospital but, with Cherie his first visitor, he eventually staged a slow and painful recovery. Booth had been on a downward spiral for quite some time, but has come out the other side. The booze has gone; the betting is in strict moderation.

"I suppose the love of racing came from my grandfather, who used to see Sceptre's owner, Bob Sievier, at the races and tell me about it. He said: 'Let the child pick out a horse!' and I chose Battleship, who won for Bruce Hobbs. I had sixpence (2½p) each-way on him at 40'1.

"My best ever National tip came from Willie Robinson in 1964. I was flying over to Ireland to film *Of Human Bondage*. It was a Sunday night and there was hardly anyone on the plane, and I thought I recognised this face at the back. Anyway I invited him into first class – the film companies looked after you in those days. We had a glass of champagne, and he told me Fulke Walwyn's Team Spirit would win the National.

Fulke Walwyn

"Later on, I bumped into him at Sandown and he told me a horse he was riding wasn't really fancied, but Fred Winter's was. I rushed through the crowd and had to dance around this tiny lady to get some 9'2. Turning to apologise, I realised it was the Queen Mother. 'You're in a hurry', she said, so I told her the story and she said she'd back it as well. And she certainly did, because I met her at the Royal Variety Performance soon afterwards and she complained she'd only got 7'2!

Tony Booth

"I started backing Team Spirit at big prices, and kept on having fivers and tenners on him, ending up with £40 each-way. But he was well beaten before Aintree and I didn't think he could possibly win, so I started looking for a saver, which was Purple Silk. I was at Liverpool for the race and I'll never forget it. On the final circuit Willie was fifth, and I kept praying he'd get get fourth to save the place money. Then it didn't matter, because Purple Silk hit the front after the last, and then, on the run-in, Team Spirit came past everything to win. It was amazing.

"Willie has been a good friend of mine ever since. After the National, you know, one or two *Sporting Life* writers wondered whether 'polished Flat jockeys' should be allowed to take on the jump boys at their own game. Willie was a hell of a rider and had finished second in the Derby on Paddy's Point."

1964 was good to Tony Booth. *Till Death*, with Warren Mitchell's appalling pater-familias Alf Garnett, was launched on an unsuspecting British public. Team Spirit did his stuff, and Labour returned to power. Whether Harold Wilson was left wing enough for the actor is another matter. Booth was offered the part of Garnett's son-in-law after being filmed heckling the Labour minister George Brown at a rally.

Halliwell's 'Filmgoers Companion' labels him: "A general purpose actor: everything from Nazis to layabouts". Better films might have arrested his frightening descent into the abyss. Or, of course, he might have stayed with Patricia Pilkington, as Pat Phoenix then was, in the early days. He is not much given to 'if onlys', but was blissfully happy when they came together again.

"She enjoyed racing, but whenever we went to the track she was mobbed," he recalled. "People were always giving her things, but no-one had ever given her a horse, so I gave her Ahona, who was trained by Nigel Tinkler. He was an Ahonoora colt, and pretty useful, too. One day at Thirsk we beat Bill O'Gorman's Provideo, who later established a juvenile record. His jockey Tony Ives told me later that was the only time they'd stepped in and had their brains on him!

"When he was older, we took Ahona to Kempton, where Nigel was due to ride him in a trainers' race, and had bundles on. We weren't very happy with the overnight box he was given, right at the far end. The bookmakers didn't mind how much they took. He ran no race and finished third, and distressed. We lost real money that afternoon.

"They were great days with the Tinklers though. I remember once at Wetherby over Christmas, the old man, Colin, was holding all this money for a hurdler Nigel was riding and the price was absolutely ridiculous, something like 4'9. Anyway, he wasn't having it and said he was going to bet 'in running'. Sure enough Nigel had it at the back, not jumping very well, and it was last of eight with a circuit to go. Three out, it was still seventh and a bookie shouted "7'2 this favourite!" and the old man was in like a flash for several grand. The horse immediately quickened up and won comfortably."

Booth, a 'proper' gambler, never allowed personal circumstances to dictate his actions. With £50 to his name at a jockeys' benevolent dinner in Newmarket, organised by the late Peter Robinson (Philip's father), he bought a £20 raffle ticket and then, as guest of honour, promptly drew it out of the hat to cries of "Fix! Fix!"

"A fortnight for two in the Bahamas and £1,000 of spending money" he recalled. "Of course, it was dead straight but I thought I'd better put it back. It was re-drawn, and the jockey Brian Jago won it. "I wouldn't have put it back," he said. As for the woman I was with, she just said, "You bloody fool!"

Which he may have been, over the years. But one who has seen a welcoming light at the end of a very long, dark tunnel. He is fun to be with again.

Nick's Much Larger Than Life

Time spent with Nick Boyd passes quickly. He works hard, plays hard and prefers to do both on the racecourse. He is a good-natured, irrepressible gambler who understands the percentages, but needs the action. Life is fun and if you have a bad run you work harder to put things right.

"I do go in for a bit of navel gazing sometimes, though," he said at Cheltenham recently. "I don't think I've ever done anything that had any real point to it."

Some of us might disagree. He served with the Army in Northern Ireland, worked on the North Sea oil rigs, ran various trendy restaurants like the Great American Disaster in Fulham and Chelsea, and hitch-hiked around the world to raise money for Action Research for the Crippled Child. Upon arriving home he appeared on the BBC programme *Tonight* and told Valerie Singleton that he'd always fancied her. Possibly playing down the wrong line there, he took his rebuff with good grace.

These days, Boyd and his wife Belinda run 20-20 Public Relations Ltd, formerly the Market Racing Agency. He acted for Carlton in their media rights bid and lists the BHB, City Index and Blue Square as other clients.

The road carrying him this far has not been without its twists and turns. "My father was in the Navy, and my first live sporting event was an Army v Navy rugby match," he recalled. "I also had my first drink on that occasion, but not my first sex. That came at an après-ski party with an Italian girl who said she was a music teacher. I'd dislocated a kneecap but we managed all right. I was brought up as a Catholic but had lapsed, rather. Anyway, it took me another two years to realise you didn't need a bandage and ski boots to do it."

But what about his first bet? "I punted quite early on. I certainly took risks and made one horrendous mistake at a City bank when quoting a price from a long out-of-date paper. It was about ten per cent too high, and suddenly the telephones were red hot. The bank lost about £250,000, which was quite a lot in 1969. I lasted a while in foreign exchange and then sold photocopiers, which was dismal, and finally opted for the Army, serving with the Royal East Anglians. But I wanted experience rather than a career so I came out and went on the oil rigs for 18 months.

"You worked two weeks on, two weeks off, and could earn £700–£900. I'd have £5 each-way on a horse, trying to win £100, not the £1,000 you'd be looking for today. We played a lot of poker and three and nine-card brag. Back in London, I was a member of the Village Casino in Sloane Street and played blackjack with Olympic swimmer David Wilkie.

"The round the world trip came about when Prince Philip suggested, in his own inimitable way, that everyone could manage it on a fiver. I drank too much one night and said I could do it," Boyd smiled. "I raised money by working as a waiter in the Great American Disaster, earning more than I used to pick up on the rigs.

Nick Boyd

"We started from the Duke of Wellington, around the corner from Eaton Square. The Duke of Wellington's son fired the gun, and Malcolm Allison's girlfriend, who worked at the Playboy Club at the time, brought the bunnies down to see us off. There was also a Brighton bookie called Nails, who drank in the pub and opened a book on how long we'd take.

"Eighteen months was favourite and we reckon he took about £2,000. He promptly did a runner, but the police took a very dim view of it and eventually caught up with him. He hasn't been seen in the south of England since." (For the record, Boyd and his American friend Thom Sandberg took 186 days, 16 hours and 45 minutes, the British and US embassies verifying their progress.)

Afterwards, Boyd ran fashionable restaurants for about 20 years. "I've always been able to take other people's ideas and work them through," he said. "But I worked long hours and then went to the casino afterwards. I play 14, 17, 20 and the neighbours on the roulette wheel, wherever I am. If I named my eight best friends, five of them would be people I've met at the tables."

There have been some wonderful moments. Fourteen red has done its bit and a Folkestone hunter-chase meeting once realised £7,500, with winners at 11'4, 33'1 and 40'1. However, his biggest gamble came unstuck.

"In 1989, Leisure Investments took over a group of restaurants I was running. They'd also bought Lingfield and I went there not just to set up a catering company for them, but also to oversee developments, like the laying of the all-weather track. But then Leisure Investments went bust and I was employed by the Receivers, Cork Gully. The fact is, I was in a position to bid for the racecourse itself. I actually slept easily on a £12m offer.

"But my principal backers were the Bank of Kuwait, an Iraqi banker and the Iraqi and Pakistani ambassadors to the Arab League. You know what happened next. Iraq's invasion of Kuwait meant all bets were off. This happened literally overnight, remember. I went white and thought I was having a heart attack. Belinda and I tried desperately to resurrect the bid and spent £65,000 trying to drum up support. But it wasn't to be, and when Trevor Hemmings took over I was unloaded as a director of Lingfield and also as managing director of Leisure Catering.

60

"I drifted for six months, frankly. But you have to get on with things. I bought a share in Gilderdale, who gave us a lot of fun, and I worked closely with advertising man Dan Abbott. The Market Racing Agency came into being, and a few years ago Skip To Somerfield became the first horse to appear in Portman Square carrying the MRA logo, when he featured in a photocall. The BHB realised what was possible, and the foundations for the Sponsorship Framework for Racehorse Owners were laid.

"The story behind Skip To Somerfield is that KP Foods had asked us to do a promotion whereby the store (it turned out to be Hounslow) which packed foods most neatly, won a horse. We leased Skippy, trained by Kevin McAuliffe, and he won at 50'1 at Kempton first time up. All the shelf-stackers and night workers were there, and the local Ladbrokes in Hounslow took a pasting!"

And so the Market Racing Agency flourished, as will 20-20 Public Relations. The whole organisation is in safe hands. Very large hands, too, because Nick Boyd is a very large man. Larger than life, you might say, and every bit as interesting.

The Poker Playing Poet

Al Alvarez describes himself as a Hampstead intellectual and no-one is about to argue. Apart from broadcasting regularly on the BBC, he has written books on subjects as diverse as suicide, mountaineering and North Sea oil. In addition, he is almost certainly the only published poet to have taken part in the World Series of poker in Las Vegas.

He is not a gambler, he insists, although Jeremy Paxman took a bit of convincing on the Radio 4 programme *Start the Week*. Let's just say Alvarez is happy in the company of gamblers, especially poker players. His new book *Poker: Bets, Bluffs, and Bad Beats* (Bloomsbury: £20.00), is a loving evocation of a twilight world – a world which unfailingly releases him from life's other cares.

There may be two more contrasting places on earth than Flask Walk, Hampstead, and Binion's Casino, Las Vegas, but they do not spring readily to mind. Alvarez, a Londoner through and through, "We had to leave Spain in 1492, but turned up here soon after Cromwell let the Jews back in in 1656," he smiles – has played poker twice a week in this country for the last 40 years, but stays at the table for days on end in Vegas. "It's what I'd do, if I didn't have to work for a living," he admits.

Not that he fools himself he would ever have a chance against the top professionals. "If you want to experience the World Series, you've got to have £10,000 you don't care about. The really good players in Vegas can spot weakness more or less straightaway. They'll be very polite about it, but they'll clean you out," he says.

Al Alvarez

At home, Alvarez played naively with a group of friends when he started out, but learned plenty from Herbert O Yardley's seminal work *The Education of a Poker Player*, published in 1957. "It taught me to play conservatively, and I won regularly at our Friday get-together for about two years. I even bought an E-type Jaguar at one point, and persuaded myself the game was easy.

"It's not, of course, and when I played in a harder school on Tuesdays I took a few beatings. I went through a very bad spell when my first marriage broke up and lost £3,000 three weeks in a row. That was a lot of money in those days and I eased off for a while."

Alvarez is quite an authority on London casinos and poker rooms. These days he plays in the Victoria Sporting Club on the Edgware Road, where there is no shortage of high rollers. "They have a £1,000 game, which means you can't sit down with less than a grand," he says. "They play Omaha and Low-ball, lots of players have £5,000 plus in front of them, and it's full.

"Texas Hold 'Em and Omaha are to ordinary five-card draw or seven-card stud what chess is to chequers. You have to get inside people's heads. I like the £100 game at the Vic, but I seldom play beyond midnight these days. After all I'm 71, so I'm in injury time! But I used to play all night in Soho, when you could go on to clubs like the Mazurka after the big casinos had closed.

"Playing late suited my lifestyle. I love literature and teaching, and after doing a research doctorate at Oxford, I could have taken a highly paid job and been made for life. But I wanted to be free to write and have always wanted to be a freelance. I started rock-climbing again at Oxford – it's my other passion – but gave up fairly recently after damaging my ankle. Part of climbing's appeal lies in the danger, although I always thought I was in control. When it comes down to it, that's the way I feel about poker, too."

Alvarez's experiences in Las Vegas in 1981 led to his first poker book *The Biggest Game In Town*, which is all about the World Series. But it was in 1994 that he actually played. *Bets, Bluffs, And Bad Beats*, as well as providing a fascinating history of the game, charts his progress. He is rather hard on himself. "I was 'tight-weak' – afraid to bet without the stone-cold nuts and easily scared out." It hurt, because he'd been waiting all his life to play against the best. When he called Anne, his wife of 35 years, she burst into tears. (Which makes a pleasant change from "I told you so".)

You end up wondering how the diverse strands of his life all came together. After all, this is a man who, in his academic life, numbered among his close friends the tragic poet Sylvia Plath. His first autobiography, *Where Did It all Go Right?* (taken from Mel Brooks' savagely funny film *The Producers*) touches on his own despair but makes it clear that things worked out all right in the end. So, did poker act as a sort of therapy? It is tempting to think so.

"I love the democracy of the poker table. Nobody gives a shit what you do or where you come from. As long as you can ante up, that's all that matters," he says. "The game changed my life, and sometimes I think it may even have saved it."

Hectic Heath Is A Man Of Many Parts

Duncan Heath, chairman of International Creative Management, is not the easiest of men to pin down. His office wall in Oxford Street W1 is covered with pictures of horses and greyhounds he has owned, but finding time to talk about them is another matter. Heath has hardly a moment to himself, which tends to be the way of it in theatrical agencies.

ICM looks after Anthony Hopkins, Rupert Everett, Catherine Zeta-Jones and Jimmy Nail, to name but a few, and the chairman points out that countless producers, scriptwriters and backroom staff are on the client list as well. "We're agents. We get them work," he said, matter of factly.

How he made a start in this hectic, unforgiving profession, where egos run high, is one of the great gambling stories of all time.

"Back in 1972 I was totally unemployable but I met a theatrical agent, a real smoothie who always seemed to have beautiful women with him. Anyway, I got a job as a gopher with the William Morris agency but was fired for gross insubordination. It was a Friday, and they gave me £100 in my hand as a pay-off.

"My mother, Joy, told me to come to Newbury races the next day, where she had Charlie Potheen running in the Hennessy. She was with a load of 'hoorays', and I remember the £100 being snatched from my hand and invested on my behalf. Charlie Potheen won, of course, and paid around 10'1 on the Tote. We all went back to Fulke Walwyn's and the celebrations continued.

"Sadly, my aunt may have overdone it because she went home, got into the bath and died. She left me £10,000 in her will, which meant I had £13,600 altogether, quite a lot for a 27-year old in 1972. I opened the Duncan Heath Agency, and ran it until ICM bought us out in 1985. And now I'm chairman of ICM."

Heath has a huge appetite for life. He co-owns a motor-cycle company and is passionate about sailing. Indeed a recent Round the Island race – the Isle of Wight, that is – meant he missed Epsom on Derby day 2000, when Supply And Demand, which he owned in partnership with screenwriter Lynda La Plante, won the opener by seven lengths under Kieren Fallon. "I asked the other crew members if I could listen to the radio commentary, and they told me to get on and do some work!" he laughed.

Duncan Heath

Heath, La Plante and Stephen Ross, her accountant, race as Action Bloodstock. "I represented Lynda as an actress, you know, but when she was sent scripts she would invariably say they were shit. So I said, 'Why don't you write them yourself?' and she did. *Widows* and *Prime Suspect* followed."

The Flat horses, including Bound For Pleasure and Freedom Stubbs, named after a character in one of La Plante's books, are trained by John Gosden these days, but Supply And Demand landed a mighty touch at Goodwood in 1998 when still with Gary Moore.

"I've also re-entered the National Hunt field, but more or less on my own," he said. "Through Cath Walwyn, Fulke's widow, I met Ben de Haan. I think he is going places as a trainer, and I don't mind how long it takes. I have two by Phardante – My Man Dan and Indian Scout – with him, plus The Piewacket (a character in *Cats*) by Rock Hopper. You could say I have the glamour with John Gosden, and the grass-roots feel with Ben. I travel to the races in the horsebox with him whenever possible."

Heath puts in a very long day. Sometimes he rises at 5 am in Earls Court (he also has a place on the Isle of Wight), drives down to Lambourn or Manton to watch the horses work, and is still at the agency soon after 9.30. And then there are the greyhounds, and all those nights at Wimbledon.

"What you must remember is this. Twenty greyhounds in training costs less than two horses. I've had some marvellous times, like watching The Plumed Ferret go up from A9 grade to A2. But Slaneyside Chief and Slaneyside Room were both heading for the Derby when they broke a hock. My plumber got me interested, and I've gone from one dog to 20 in a year!"

Heath habitually backs his greyhounds in £100 doubles, trebles or accumulators in the William Hill shop across the road. "Yes, I know it's optimistic. My accountant (who rejoices in the name of Mr. Doshi) thought so too, and suggested I tone it down a bit. Unfortunately, he made the point just before three of them went in at 7'1, 9'1 and 16'1. How much did that cost me?"

I told him I made the treble £136,000, but pointed out that Hills would have smashed the 16'1 shot through the floorboards, so it wouldn't have been that much. He still rang Mr. Doshi to pass on a few random thoughts.

He was married to Hilary Dwyer, who starred in *Hadleigh* with Gerald Harper but gave up acting when the first agency was set up. Amicably divorced, the couple's children are Daniel, studying at the Berklee College of Music in Boston, and Laura, about to renounce acting in favour of a veterinary assistant's job at Battersea Dogs' Home.

Heath is happy with his lot. "I started betting as a very young man," he remarked, "but these days I don't bet much outside my own horses, because I'm just too busy with the agency. And I can tell you this: there is *nothing* as exciting as standing in the winner's enclosure".

His telephones start ringing again, but there was time for one final observation. "When you're on your deathbed, will you be thinking about your share portfolio, or the horse you should have entered for the Cheltenham Gold Cup?" he said.

After half an hour in Duncan Heath's company, the answer comes to you fairly quickly.

nine

The Whirling Dervish Of Pound Tree Road

The first Stewards' Cup I remember with any clarity is Skymaster's triumph in 1961. I wish I could recall Ashurst Wonder bursting clear in 1954, but I was only five at the time. People in Southampton spoke of trainer Les Hall in hushed tones, and when I was old enough to comprehend what had happened, which must have been all of six months later, I readily accepted the romantic notion that that the wind had blown Ashurst Wonder home. He had only 6st 11lb on his back.

Jockeys really were that small. I developed a fascination for senior riders who could manage 7st 7lb. David East, with his funny red cheeks, riding Antiquarian for Herbert Blagrave. Ray Reader on Patient Constable. Sammy ("I know people in racing and they tell me things") Millbanks, in his later role as a tipster. L.C. Parkes and Norman McIntosh. Norman rode for George Boyd, but missed out when Rockavon won the 1961 2000 Guineas, because Norman Stirk rode that day.

George was easy to please and let anyone get up on his horses, as long as they came from Scotland, could do the weight and were called Norman.

I love Goodwood for all manner of reasons. It sits a stone's throw from my favourite stretch of coast, there are enough sprint handicaps to keep a masochist happy, and the Brighton Evening

Argus turns up towards the end of each day's racing at the big July meeting.

Then you can wait for the traffic to ease and work out whether to go to Hove or Portsmouth greyhounds to put things right. Unless you've bought tickets for Chekhov's *The Cherry Orchard* at Chichester Theatre, of course. (It's a good choice. They come close to losing everything in that, too.)

If you go to Portsmouth dogs in Target Road you can find a guest house in Southsea afterwards and sit outside, looking at the fairy lights. They're exactly like the ones in Franco Brusati's film *Dimenticare Venezia*, where everyone goes off to Venice at the end except for the central character, who sits down, loosens his belt, sips a glass of wine and wonders how everything got away from him. He had bigger worries than solving the Stewards' Cup.

I wish I'd been at Goodwood in 1878, when the extraordinary mare Kincsem won the Goodwood Cup on her only visit to England. Kincsem was Hungarian-bred and won all 54 of her races in five different countries. Horses were for the racing in those days. Kincsem was as hard as nails on the track but a complete softie otherwise. She never travelled anywhere unless her favourite cat was in the box.

Sentiment often plays a part in racing. I wish I had a £10 note for every time someone has started humming a tune in the Tote queue because the name of one of the horses was the same as a popular song. In just over 40 years I have never backed a winner under these circumstances.

When I was young a horse called Only You ran at Goodwood. They were all singing it. "Only you can make this change in me. For it's true you are my destiny. When you hold my hand, I understand the magic that you do. You're my dream come true, my one and only you."

Finished third, unfortunately. The closest I ever came was with the cleverly named sprinter Crowded Avenue, who features in 'I Only Have Eyes For You.'

> *I don't know if we're in a garden,*
> *Or on some crowded avenue.*
> *You are here, so am I,*

Maybe millions of people go by,
But they all disappear from view -
And I only have eyes for you.

Crowded Avenue was by Sizzling Melody. Whenever he ran at Goodwood, I used to stand in the Tote queue and hum 'I Only Have Eyes For You', but he deteriorated and ended up in Sandown claimers, so I gave up.

Although the Stewards' Cup fascinates me, I had rather more luck in the sixties with a lovely old mare called Nicolina, who was more effective in a similar, though less competitive, sprint handicap later in the week. Often she achieved very little in the course of the season but came good on the Friday of the Glorious meeting, much to the delight of this writer, then a boardman in a Ladbrokes' shop in Pound Tree Road, Southampton.

The Odeon cinema was opposite Pound Tree Road and I remember going to see *Sodom And Gomorrah* there. Funny how we used to queue around the block to see the sort of things available in any newsagents today. It was an odd film and went on for ages, though not as long as *Exodus*, which had been running for three hours when the Jewish comedian Mort Sahl stood up at the preview and said to Otto Preminger "Otto – let my people go!"

Sodom and Gomorrah were rich, sinful cities and seemed to be doing all right until Lot and the Hebrews turned up. I was never a big Stewart Granger fan, although he was all right in *Scaramouche*. As for Stanley Baker, well, you can't wear a white mac with the collar turned up in a biblical epic, so he struggled a bit. He was best in *Blind Date*, where he played a London copper with a streaming head cold the whole way through. That was a nice touch, and it wasn't as if he had any intimate scenes to get through, not in 1959, because sex wasn't invented for another four years.

In those pre-SIS, very much Extel blower commentary days, my style in the saddle was much admired in Pound Tree Road as I began riding a finish as soon as the commentator picked out Nicolina. Her trainer, Roy Pettitt, fell on hard times and sold a story to *The Sun*, saying that he livened her up with something illegal in time for the Goodwood race. I didn't believe a word of it. She just came good at around the same time every year. I believe and disbelieve what suits me. I don't believe George Gershwin is dead, for example.

Racing at Goodwood used to start in the morning. On the third and final day of the meeting in 1802, the City of Chichester Stakes was run in heats over three miles. A five-year old called Mystery won the first two heats straight off and was declared the outright winner after only six miles. There was no need for him to run in the final heat.

Do you know who owned him? A banker called Mr Ladbroke. I like to think there's a message there for all of us.

ten

The Genius Of Piggott

The best place to celebrate Lester Piggott's second retirement is probably Dublin. That's where they talk about genius and leave out the 'flawed' bit.

If I were that good at something, I could live with a few flaws. It's having the flaws *without* being a genius that stings.

"Unless you're in the know, there's no straight sport now. Lenehan gets some good ones. He's giving Sceptre today. Zinfandel's the favourite, Lord Howard de Walden's. Won at Epsom."

That is from Joyce's *Ulysses,* as Leopold Bloom continues his journey across the city with a visit to Davy Byrne's bar. Zinfandel won the Ascot Gold Cup in 1905 when the late Lord Howard's father, happily ensconced beneath a tree in the paddock, is said to have contemplated the score for an opera. He wrote the libretto for at least three highly successful productions.

"Malacca was tipped to win at Harold's Cross, rumours about Yellow Printer's limitations were denied. At Brighton, the £35 filly Qalibashi had won at 20'1. Whisky Poker was selected for the 3.00 at Redcar, and Whisky Noggin for the 3.30. Privy Seal would win at Ascot.

"Eugene sat, considering a few of the facts he had absorbed, listening to the ticking of the clock. Within a couple of minutes

Lester Piggott

his head dropped on to his chest and he returned to sleep. He snored softly; he dreamed he was standing in Riordan's public house."

An excerpt from *Mrs. Eckdorf in O'Neills Hotel,* first published in 1969. When John Meacock named all of his horses after Persian heroes and places, I wonder what odds you could have had about one of them appearing in a novel by William Trevor?

Until the recent spate of 'Glaswegian' novels, several of which revolve around the tenement, the pub and the betting office, the subject of racing was far more likely to crop up in works by serious Irish writers than anywhere else.

Racing was an everyday topic, in this bar and that. It is no great surprise that Lester remains a god in the Emerald Isle, and if there had been a way of organising one final ride, they would have queued up overnight to say their goodbyes.

Everyone has his favourite Piggott memory. Thank heaven he got beat on Pretty Puffin in the First Day Supplementary Plate on Cheveley Park day in October, 1969.

Running out of the Dip, Eric Eldin was about half a length to the good on Gaykart, and the great man was winding himself up for a Roberto-style finish on the favourite. Even now I don't know how Eric stayed in front, but there was still a neck in it at the line. Newmarket, as cold and bleak as ever, with a bruised autumnal sky glowering only a couple of minutes earlier, was suddenly the perfect place to witness the glorious changing of the seasons. All it needed was some Vivaldi on the tannoy. £30 was a lot of money in 1969.

Of course, I also remember Nijinsky in the St. Leger. He was some way below his best that day after an attack of ringworm, but the racing press was so determined to write him up as a superstar that it readily took Piggott's nonchalant performance at face value.

In fact, Meadowville would have made things very difficult for this charismatic racehorse with a little further to travel, but Lester could always make it look as if he was coasting.

When he won the Leger again on Commanche Run his injured leg was sticking out at an odd angle all the way up the straight. If you look back at the film of that race, there are two or three occasions when Baynoun looks absolutely certain to go past.

And Baynoun and Steve Cauthen give everything, but still can't quite manage it. Cauthen, due to ride in America the next day, is still shaking his head on the plane hours afterwards. "That Lester," he keeps saying, "he's just *different*".

Some of the stories about him are apocryphal, and some have been embellished over the years, but I can vouch for at least two.

Before Teenoso's King George, I was worried about asking for an interview because I was pretty sure BBC Radio still owed him for one the previous autumn. He arrived at Ascot carrying a huge suitcase and bumped into Geoffrey Summers, former secretary of the Jockeys' Association.

"Hello, Lester," said Geoffrey. "I didn't know you were going on to Warwick afterwards."

"Oh no, Geoffrey," he replied, "I thought it was about time I collected the money for all these interviews I've been doing. That fellow Carnaby owes fifty quid for a start".

And he never allowed a loose opinion to go unchallenged. I thought an interview was going pretty well one day, and suggested that Ardross was catching Akiyda towards the end of the 1982 Arc.

He gave me that piercing, almost pitying look. "Yeah. If we'd gone round again," he said. "Yves was just playing with me, you know?"

I miss interviewing him, even though it unfailingly made me nervous. The point is, with Lester you really shouldn't mind being the fall guy. And when he returned to race-riding after the first retirement, it seemed a good idea to me, because I believe any man should be allowed to combat boredom in the way that suits him best.

I never thought he was as good as before (how could he be?) but seeing him in action did not occasion sadness in the way that, for example, watching George Best play for Fulham had done.

We should enjoy our heroes for as long as we can, and with Lester we were darned lucky to have a second bite at the cherry.

It is something they almost certainly understand better across the Irish Sea.

eleven

Seeing Bessie Smile – Short Story, 2004

The bike that Bessie had set her heart on, but did not expect to receive, was £172. Arthur knew this because she had pointed it out to him the week before in High Holborn. It was a smart red job, the sort her friends would be riding on Christmas morning. Arthur, with five days left, had exactly £89.50.

Tiring suddenly of the throng in Oxford Street, he wandered across Covent Garden and sat in Nell of Old Drury, opposite the theatre. Years ago, when he trod the boards without attracting critical acclaim, Arthur had watched a now-famous actor reading a script in the Nell, waiting for the right moment to play the fruit machine.

He was probably holding about £2, and won almost straightaway. From the brief clatter, Arthur put it at around a tenner. The actor counted it, pocketed it, took it out and counted it again. Ordered another half. Arthur, six figures adrift these many years, nodded approval. All true gamblers have counted coins, not notes, at some stage.

Arthur loved Bessie with a dull ache. She was his only child, and certain to remain so. An unkind man might have said she was a bit heavy for her 12 years, and Arthur knew early on that she was a bit slow. Just a tiny bit. She'd be up with the maths homework when the others had gone to bed, and he dreaded the day it would all drift beyond him. Algebra, geometry, parallel lines and arrows, all the rest of it. But for the moment she got there eventually with his help, and Arthur would murmur "Well done, Bessie," and her face would light up. He lived for her smile.

A recovering whisky alcoholic, Arthur never considered total abstinence and sipped halves of bitter. Looking out at the shoppers in the weak December light, he went over the figures again. Next dole payment, first week in January. Next hand-out from the Bear and Staff, where he worked as a barman (no questions asked), the Friday after Christmas. The van safely parked in a garage alongside King's Cross, where he knew the owner, who'd built things up again after losing his stash at Walthamstow dogs.

It was all about will power in the end. Arthur knew a bookmaker who'd been absolutely hammered on Dettori day at Ascot and had to sell sheets of Christmas paper in Oxford Street, just to keep himself and his family afloat. Actually standing there on the corner, he was. He'd sworn Arthur to secrecy, which was never a problem. Anyway, he was all right again now, larger than life in fact, and Arthur wondered why punters couldn't see there was a message there somewhere.

£89.50, less the half of bitter he was drinking in this nice old gaff, with the bar staff in floppy Father Christmas hats and the shop girls giggling over dry white wine. How do you know when you're middle-aged? Young women find you invisible. Unless you become very rich or famous, of course, in which case some of them find you very visible indeed. Funny old game.

Just after 12.45pm. The Quare Fellow due off at 1.30 in a novice chase at Ludlow. £70 to win, couldn't be less than 6'4, maybe 13'8. £175 plus the balance of what he was holding. The Coral shop in Covent Garden, the walk in the fading light to King's Cross, the van back to Holborn, the bike, the drive to Wandsworth in heavy traffic, no hardship at all, the bike safely lodged with Kevin in the Bear. If these sums were correct, which they undoubtedly were, there was enough to buy Maureen some lilies on Christmas Eve. Oriental lilies. Not enough to ease the bitter disappointment of the choices she'd made in life, one of them being Arthur, but the right sort of gesture nonetheless.

Or, of course, there was the tube due west to Beauchamp Place and the Melrose. Because Arthur wasn't going home without the bike, even if The Quare Fellow lost.

It involved seeing Louise, and asking her, which was just about the last thing on earth he wanted, but he'd do it. And she'd say yes, in that quizzical, slightly mocking way. Arthur had done things in his life of which he was none too proud, but he'd never asked a woman for money before. He'd need £200, and no-one else would lend him that much. He had no credit and no plastic. It was a battle between his self-respect and seeing Bessie smile, and self-respect would have to wait.

Christmas spirit had failed lamentably to cheer the regulars in the Coral shop. A forlorn task, even a depressing one, Arthur thought. Sleigh bells ring, are you listening? Not around here, apparently. The Quare Fellow was 7'4, Tell Me Sarah 9'4 and the others pretty easy to back.

The Quare Fellow was a quick, clean hurdler who put in the occasional short one over fences. The mare was a willing plodder who would take advantage of any mistakes he made. Arthur wrote out the slip and took the 7'4. Nothing changed, except that she eased out to 5'2. And, as his heart started thumping because he'd never held his daughter's Christmas happiness in his hands before, they were off and running and Tell Me Sarah fell at the first.

Arthur stared at the screen. She got up and cantered off. Gardiner on The Quare Fellow glanced over his shoulder and pushed on steadily, gradually increasing the tempo as the motley crew behind struggled to stay in touch. Sweat trickled from Arthur's armpits on this cool December day. He thought of walking around the block, going to a different shop, looking sideways at some other screen somewhere else, going back to the Nell, ringing Racecall when it was bound to be over, but did none of these things.

The Quare Fellow met the third last in his stride and quickened away from it a fence clear. He was sent off at 13'8, not 7'4, the screen said. Surprise, surprise, Arthur thought. And then, with Bessie squealing and hugging him in delight, he saw the horse bearing hard to his left with Gardiner frantically pulling his whip through to set him straight. Sometimes you win too easily, often you don't win at all. The Quare Fellow swerved right across to the wing and stopped dead, hurling Gardiner out of the side door. The jockey sat on the ground, shaking his head in disbelief as the horse trotted away. The camera had still to pick up any of those sweating it out for a place. Arthur, who would have given a year of his life never to have been a gambler, found a new level of despair. Walking straight out, he cursed loudly and profanely, his impressive oath prompting a mixture of contempt and curiosity among those waiting patiently for the Wednesday matinee at the Theatre Royal.

Louise, on the point of an amicable divorce, was more sophisticated than Maureen and had tried her level best to take Arthur away from her. He never really knew why, although Louise, who ran a small antiques shop in Wandsworth, loved the theatre and was always asking about minor roles he'd played when everything still looked possible. In the Bear, the men wondered what she'd be like, the way they do, and there came a time when Arthur could have told them. But talking too much was never one of his weaknesses.

Although he did not love Louise, he was utterly obsessed by her. It was an ongoing sickness involving lost afternoons and lies, and the more he thought it was bound to end the more he woke up in the night, thinking of her again. Then he would slip out of bed and pour himself a large one, re-awakening a love affair with scotch which had blossomed in his early twenties. Soon he was looking for a 'livener' in the mornings, as well. The telephone rang less frequently, then not at all. A good-looking man of no mean ability but no real drive, he was all washed up.

The only way things could change was for Maureen to find out about Louise, and someone duly told her. He came home one afternoon when she should still have been at work at the library and found her sitting on the stairs with his suitcase packed. Bessie, two at the time, was screaming at the top of her voice, her face flushed and streaked with tears. Maureen, dry-eyed, looked at him with contempt. "Must be quite a girl, your fancy tart. I don't know how she can stand the smell," she said.

So he started on the long road back. He told Louise the next morning it was over, putting up with words like 'weak' and 'pathetic' for a while but holding firm. The thought of Bessie being brought up by someone else saved him, although it was another three years before he gave up the whisky.

The tube clattered towards Knightsbridge. Arthur knew that Louise had remarried after leaving Wandsworth and that her husband owned two or three smart wine bars. One or two regulars in the Bear said that she ran the Melrose for him and Arthur had chanced a telephone call when working out his plan. The husky voice was unmistakeable and Arthur felt the same old feeling welling up inside him. He put the receiver down.

Sometimes he wondered what sort of man Bessie would find attractive. Someone straight and reliable, he thought. Looks not too important. In his mind's eye he saw her as a nursery teacher. When he watched her in the playground the younger children were generally all around her, looking for guidance. Bessie was an old 12, really. An organiser, like her mother. Arthur had nearly lost two organisers.

It should have been later, but it was still only three o'clock. They were holding the bike in the High Holborn shop until 5.30. There were two things about the Melrose that he couldn't have known, though one he might have suspected. The cheapest glass of white wine was £5.50, so he had enough for two but not three. And he'd have to offer Louise one while he worked round to the request. If she was there today.

He'd thought of lying about a damaged credit card being swallowed by the machine, but it wouldn't wash. The banks were still open and he'd have been able to sort something out. He was just going to let the conversation take its course, wait for her to ask what was wrong – his expression making it pretty obvious that something was – and he was going to say: "Actually, I'm struggling a bit for Christmas". Those exact words. Then he saw how busy the bar was with Christmas shoppers and his spirits sank.

The second thing concerned the ambience of the place. Yes, it was smart, all right. But it was also perfectly obvious that racing people were specially catered for. Prints of Sir Ivor and Nijinsky around the walls, that famous black and white picture of Piggott, face all lined and drawn, cartoons, jokes and a framed copy of the last *Sporting Life* ever printed.

───────────

Arthur sat down on the one available bar stool and ordered a glass of Muscadet. When he saw her almost immediately, talking to a group of businessmen at the far end, he thought briefly that his heart might stop altogether. She was slightly greyer but still stunningly attractive, and when she turned to give the bar staff some instructions it would have given the boys in the Bear plenty to wonder about all over again.

And in that moment Arthur felt spent and used and realised how ridiculous his quest had been. She would see him and come over, but there would be no privacy, no time, no way of bringing the conversation round. And there would be no bike, of course, not for a few weeks anyway, and Bessie would swallow her disappointment as so often in the past.

"Any luck today?" A well-dressed old boy with a London Standard had materialised at his side.

Blimey, they must all be punters in here, Arthur thought. "No, no good. I fancied a horse called The Quare Fellow but he let me down. You know the way it is," he said, looking at the door. He felt grubby and out of place and didn't want her to see him now.

His companion looked puzzled. "The Quare Fellow? That won, didn't it? Nothing got round and Billy Gardiner went and rounded him up. Finished alone. Only just in time, mind. Buy you a drink?"

Arthur stared at him. The words hung in the air, not finding any takers. Half a minute went by. "I say, tell me to mind my own business but you look a bit pale, old chap. Do you want a whisky or something?"

And Arthur could not find the words but took the old boy's hand and grasped it firmly. At last he said: "No, you're very kind but I'm all right now. There's a glass of Muscadet coming which I'd like you to have. I really must get back to Covent Garden quite quickly". Old habits die hard, and he knew the slip was safe in his back pocket.

When he turned at the door she was still talking to the businessmen, laughing in that husky, throaty way he would take with him to the grave but never hear again for real.

And then the tears were stinging his eyes and he was running all the way back up to Knightsbridge, pausing only to pay over the odds for a few sheets of Christmas paper. Might come in handy for the oriental lilies, he thought.

twelve

Trains Of Thought, 1997

All I know about modern trains is that they fizz at both ends. This is just as well, because the one I'm on at 7am has broken down at Didcot Parkway.

It has to do a sort of three-point turn, taking in Reading, Oxford and Swindon. Thus the fizzy bit which works is at the front, but we are all travelling backwards. I hurtle towards Nailsea taking in parts of Bedminster I never knew existed.

When I presented a programme on HTV West, the station controller used to say, "Always imagine you're broadcasting to the little old lady in Bedminster". Well, I think I've just seen her. She's tottering up past a Chinese restaurant which also does fish and chips. She must be really old now, because I've been gone for ten years. If this train hadn't been going backwards, I'd have missed her.

They couldn't turn trains round in the old days because there was no fizzy bit at the back. But I miss the little man who used to jump down and swing the water pump across while the engine panted in anticipation.

I think *Bude* was 34006, West Country Class on the old Southern Region. Actually I don't just think that, I'd have a thumping good bet on it if someone laid me a price. That's the trouble these days, you can't get on. I've ended up needing some

itinerant, insomniac bookmaker wandering up and down the carriage saying, "Even money *Bude* to be 34006. Who wants it?"

This train has gone backwards all the way through Bristol, from Parkway to Temple Meads, and the Indian conductor keeps on apologising. I don't know why, because I'm the only person on it, and I'm not complaining.

I doubt that an English conductor would keep apologising if we were approaching Bombay the wrong way round. Not that Nailsea can be compared to Bombay, of course, despite recent culinary departures.

This Indian chap doesn't remember the old steam days. I keep testing him. 34092? Complete silence. *City of Wells,* I think.

34008? Baffled smile. *Padstow,* unless I'm much mistaken. I can see he wants to fire some Indian engine numbers at me, but he's too polite.

Apparently there is flooding between Stapleton Road and Filton Junction. Flooding! And you were worried about firm ground at Cheltenham. All trains are subject to delays, the Indian man says. Even the ones going backwards.

I went to Bude this week, to see Walter Dennis and his wife Jill.

The rain is coming in time for Coome Hill, and I think he will win everything. I was thinking I wouldn't have a bet until Ken Ivory runs Never Think Twice in the first sprint handicap at Folkestone, but the Dennis family are lovely people and now I'm backing Coome Hill for the Gold Cup and the Martell Grand National.

I took my little girl to Bude and she ran up and down the beach in the wind and rain. Graham Greene was right: once you love you're vulnerable. Sometimes you ache for people not to get any older. Children don't care about it being winter or summer, which is a good reason for not growing up. Not that some of us need a reason.

I went to the Dorchester for the National weights lunch on Tuesday. I sat next to Cornelius Lysaght before he went round with the 'mic', interviewing all the trainers. I couldn't do it myself unless I'd had a few large ones and all the trainers were Josh Gifford or David Nicholson.

As I may have mentioned before, Lysaght is some performer, scurrying around the place, talking himself through it, shuffling his notes and still finding a riposte when someone slips in an unscheduled remark. I know how difficult it is and he deserves congratulations.

I should think the Martell lunch is quite a novelty at the Dorchester, because it's the only time there are any English people in there. I went and sat in the foyer afterwards and listened to the pianist.

> *Someday he'll come along, the man I love:*
> *And he'll be big and strong, the man I love.*

And almost certainly from the Middle East, I should think, if you're waiting for it to happen in Park Lane.

Oh dear. This train has shot through Nailsea backwards and is on its way to Weston-super-Mare. I must say I never realised there were so many allotments in Yatton. I've never been to Weston-super-Mare station before. There are some interesting posters outside the waiting room saying: 'For the Wages Of Sin Is Death'. I wonder if they take that down before the illicit weekenders turn up. Enjoy yourselves, but don't forget the wages of sin is death. And watch out for the man from the *News of the World*.

I suppose I ought to write some of this down. No, let's not bother. Let's go and play with the little one on the beach at Bude while there's still time.

thirteen

A Little Light Reading

I thought I might use this space to write about short stories, and the part racing has played in them. The two best racing tales are, perhaps, *Tip On A Dead Jockey* by Irwin Shaw, and *My Old Man* by Ernest Hemingway. Like the best of Hugh McIlvanney's pieces, *My Old Man* would win prizes outside the narrow confines of sport.

My top five short stories are:

The Dead, by James Joyce
The Rich Boy, by F Scott Fitzgerald
My Old Man, by Ernest Hemingway
Tip On A Dead Jockey, by Irwin Shaw
and *The Swimmer*, by John Cheever.

Only the two mentioned earlier are about racing. But I believe the others would hold your attention, especially *The Rich Boy*, in which Fitzgerald sketches a character, Anson Hunter, not so very different from Jay Gatsby.

As one who believes the class system is alive and well and will comfortably see us under the sod, I like Fitzgerald's description of the rich. "They think, deep in their hearts, that they are better than we are because we had to discover the compensations and refuges of life for ourselves. Even when they enter deep into our world or sink below us, they still think that they are better than we are. They are different." (When he read this, Hemingway said, "Of course they're different. They're richer.")

Anson is thwarted in love and drinks too much. Fitzgerald knew all about that, of course, as well as the onset of alcoholic remorse. "If you had overdone it and your heart was slightly out of order, you went on the wagon for a few days without saying anything about it, and waited until an accumulation of nervous boredom projected you into another party."

I'm not sure what made me think of *The Rich Boy*, although Julian Wilson's unintentionally amusing piece in the *Racing Post* about exchange betting, and the heartfelt wish that the *hoi polloi* should push off and leave proper betting to people with middle names like Bonhote, possibly had something to do with it.

Anson, never quite the same after seeing his lover happily married to someone else, goes on a cruise. Inevitably, there are other women "to nurse and protect that superiority he cherished in his heart". Racing knows a few people like that.

My Old Man

Hemingway is not everyone's cup of tea and his macho world of huntin', shootin' and fishin' can sometimes be wearin'. But it's good to know that one of the best short stories ever written is about racing, and anyone who cannot enjoy *My Old Man* is highly unlikely to fall in love with the turf.

Seen through the eyes of an impressionable adolescent, the son of a journeyman American jockey drifting towards the end of his career, here are the racetracks of Milan and Paris, the hustlers and smooth operators, the early-morning sweat, the boulevards, the papers, the gossip, the chewing of the fat over endless rounds of coffee, and the way adults seem to kids in a magical world.

San Siro on a perfect day. "I was nuts about the horses, too. There's something about it, when they come out and go up the track to the post. Sort of dancy and tight-looking with the jock keeping a tight hold on them and maybe easing off a little and letting them run a little going up. Then once they were at the barrier it got me worse than anything. Especially at San Siro with that big green infield and the mountains way off and the fat wop starter with his big whip and the jocks fiddling them around."

It's wonderful stuff. No-one ever used repetition as effectively as Papa, and no-one ever will again. Can you read that and not want to be at San Siro?

Apart from anything else, *My Old Man* is a coming of age story with a tragic ending. Things are not quite as they seem, a chance remark takes the shine off a perfect day, innocence ebbs away. The champion, War Cloud, is supposed to win a big race in Paris but doesn't quite, and the kid's old man murmurs, "George Gardner's a swell jockey all right. It sure took a great jock to keep that War Cloud from winning".

"Of course I knew it was funny all the time. But my old man saying it right out like that sure took the kick all out of it for me and I didn't get the real kick back again ever."

Love, pain and death in France and Italy. If you were trying to show someone how a short story should be written, you might as well hand them *My Old Man* and say nothing at all.

Paris Blues

It would be unfair to compare Irwin Shaw with either Hemingway or Fitzgerald. He has rather slipped out of fashion, which is a pity, and it's high time television found an afternoon slot for *Two Weeks In Another Town*, which has not been on for a while.

He wrote short stories for the better part of 50 years and there are some gems among them, including another Parisian racing tale, *Tip On A Dead Jockey*. This was also made into a film starring Robert Taylor, but it didn't work – often the way of it when Hollywood takes hold of an excellent story which is nonetheless too slight to fill a couple of hours.

Masochists have a soft spot for Lloyd Barber, an American in the French capital, down on his luck but handed a chance to turn things around. Unfortunately, it's a no questions asked job for the former flier, and Barber is never short of questions.

Tip On A Dead Jockey turns on a steeplechase at Auteuil, after which Barber will give his answer regarding the proposed mission. Prompted by 'Bert Smith', the suave individual holding the money for this venture, which is almost certainly illegal, he backs number 5, a mare trying fences for the first time.

Given that the jockey will be killed when she comes down at the fourth, there is something dispassionate in Shaw's appraisal of the horse and rider combination in the parade ring. But then, Barber, a gloomy pragmatist, has been up against it for a long time and sees things as they are.

"Her jockey was a man of about forty, with a long, scooped French nose. He was an ugly man, and when he opened his mouth, you saw that most of his front teeth were missing. Barber, looking at him, thought, it's too bad such ugly men get to ride such beautiful animals."

All but the most disciplined gamblers believe in omens and, from the moment Barber looks through the glasses and sees the jockey's crumpled, motionless form, he will not be flying the mission. "He closed his eyes altogether and saw the maps spread out on the bed in his room. The Mediterranean. The wide reaches of open water. He remembered the smell of burning. The worst smell. The smell of your dreams during the war. The smell of hot metal, smouldering rubber. Smith's tip."

How things turn out need not concern us here, but Shaw captures perfectly that moment when a main chance comes and goes. We know it's a main chance, we can reach out and take it, and life may never be the same again. But, like Barber, we stay in our seat, and sip another scotch, and let it go. We settle for the routineness of tomorrow.

Big Burt And The American Dream

Burt Lancaster made some thoughtful films during his career and, unlike many of his colleagues, was not averse to taking the odd risk. *The Train* (1964), for example, which had Nazi Paul Scofield trying to spirit away French art treasures in 1944, was made in black and white and went on for 2 hours 20 minutes! (Imagine that today.)

But the real curiosity was *The Swimmer*, made four years later, with Burt in his trunks the whole time and swimming home via the pools of his rich friends. Like a lot of things we don't understand, it turns out to be about the failure of the American Dream, just as any British film which left us in the dark 15 years ago was "a metaphor for Thatcher's Britain".

The Swimmer sort of stays with you, though, so I went and bought John Cheever's short story and found it quite harrowing. Because, as Neddy Merrill moves from pool to pool, from this boisterous Sunday party to that, it becomes clear that not everyone is pleased to see him. In fact, one or two hostesses seem to expect him to ask for money, while another, a former mistress, informs him curtly that she is entertaining. And he can't even remember how long ago it was they had their affair. Arriving home exhausted, the garage door is rusty, the house is locked and the rooms are empty. And it dawns on the reader that Neddy is slowly losing his mind and is something of an embarrassment to his glitzy, shallow neighbours.

An extraordinary piece, but not about racing, I admit, and nor is James Joyce's *The Dead*, though I was reminded the other day that, when my luck turns, I'd like to buy and name a filly The Lass Of Aughrim.

When you think of the major, blockbuster movies John Huston made – *The African Queen, The Asphalt Jungle, The Man Who Would Be King* – it seems strange that, late in life, he turned to Joyce's gentle tale of a Dublin Christmas party where Gabriel Conroy, happy and successful, and with nothing more to worry about than his prepared thanksgiving speech, is suddenly made aware that his wife may once have nursed a grand passion.

Who was it who said, "People don't change because we discover more about them. They were always like that, but we've only just found out"?

Gretta Conroy is stopped quite literally in her tracks when another guest, the wonderfully named Mr Bartell d'Arcy, sings a verse or two of 'The Lass of Aughrim', the favourite song of a boy who died at 17.

Gabriel "tried to keep up his tone of cold interrogation but his voice when he spoke was humbled and indifferent".

"I suppose you were in love with this Michael Furey, Gretta," he said.

"I was great with him at that time," she said.

"And what did he die of so young, Gretta? Consumption, was it?"

"I think he died for me," she answered. "He was ill at the time in his lodgings in Galway and wouldn't be let out and his people in Oughterard were written to. And when I was only a week in the convent he died and he was buried in Oughterard where his people came from. O, the day I heard that, that he was dead!"

And the conclusion. "Yes, the newspapers were right: snow was general all over Ireland. It was falling on every part of the dark central plain, on the treeless hills, falling softly upon the Bog of Allen and, farther westward, softly falling into the dark mutinous Shannon waves. It was falling, too, upon every part of the lonely churchyard on the hill where Michael Furey lay buried. It lay thickly drifted on the crooked crosses and headstones, on the spears of the little gate, on the barren thorns. His soul swooned slowly as he heard the snow falling faintly through the universe and faintly falling, like the descent of their last end, upon all the living and the dead."

By God, imagine if we could write like that. Still, a filly called The Lass Of Aughrim would be handsome compensation.

fourteen

Love In The Afternoon – Short Story, 1996

I'm Billy Danruthers. You look at me and think, "I've seen that chap before," and you probably have, because I trod the boards for a long time. Drawing room comedies, mostly. I was the slightly older best friend the main character could always turn to in times of trouble. Wry sense of humour, grey at the temples, time for a gin and tonic. You've got the picture.

I sang in the Chesterfield Hotel when I was resting. Old standards like 'Our Love is Here to Stay', that was my favourite. My wives had very little in common, but they all said I gambled too much and was born too late. Then they tended to settle for someone who was born even later, but we won't go into that.

When the work dried up I'd drift across London – a *flaneur*, as the French say – visiting old haunts and making notes for a fading showbiz magazine. They had a picture of me in a smoking jacket, from the time I was in *Private Lives* or *Bitter Sweet*, I can't remember which. Let's face it, when you've seen one of Noel's plays…

Anyway, I'd start the day in The Grapes, in Shepherd Market, or sometimes the Victoria, just off Hyde Park Corner, and read *The Sporting Life* from cover to cover before the lunchtime crowd came in. Then I'd place my bets and wander over to Covent Garden.

You'd see a face or two in the Marquess of Anglesea near Drury Lane, especially when there was a matinee on, so I'd listen and jot things down and they all absolutely *loved* it, as you can well imagine.

What I remember most clearly about the day in question is the heat. When I arrived at the Victoria the sun-worshippers were already out in force in the park, and there was barely a space to be had. Two of my wives loved the sun. "You're such an autumn sort of a person, aren't you Billy?" one of them said, although I've no idea what she meant.

Folkestone was on that day, and Gavin Pritchard-Gordon had Powder River Grey in the seller. I was familiar with all of his horses, having had shares in one or two when things were going rather better. I must have been deeply into the form of this selling race, because Alfie startled me when he spoke. "How do you bet?" he said.

I was never quite sure what Alfie did for a living, but he was always in the Victoria and seemed to know everyone. He had this disconcerting habit of introducing me to complete strangers as if they were bound to recognise me, and getting a real kick out of it when they didn't.

I preferred Brendan, who said absolutely nothing for hours on end but then sat bolt upright and shouted, "Pandofell! Ascot Gold Cup! Lester Piggott up!" before lapsing into silence again. The race had been run more than 30 years before, and Alfie said it was probably the last winner Brendan had backed.

"What does Billy think?" Henry asked.

"Can't make contact with him," Alfie replied. "I believe he's sussing one out."

There was much merriment around the bar. I wish Alfie wouldn't give people ammunition like that. "Gavin Pritchard Gordon's has a chance," I said. "What do I think about what?"

Alfie grinned and nodded towards a couple sitting about six bar stools along. They were a short, middle-aged Australian tourist, fairly voluble, and a girl at least 30 years his junior who looked rather more local. She wasn't really sitting on the stool; she was perched on it, in quite the shortest dress I'd seen since the sixties.

And I'd seen her in there before, maybe a couple of years ago. She looked utterly stunning, both times.

Arnold, the mechanic, was sweating slightly. It really was very hot. "So?" he said.

"Look, I'm no expert, but I'd say there's no betting," I said. "It's a long time since I've seen it happening in the middle of the day, but this place has always been very tolerant and discreet." I picked up the paper again.

There was a long silence, broken eventually by Henry. He is so quiet and dignified. He loaded his pipe, tamping it down the way they do, and murmured, "I think you're wrong, old chap."

"Could easily be," I agreed. "Geoff Lewis has got one in there which didn't run too badly last time. I like old Gavin, though. Perhaps I'll ring him up and see what he thinks."

"No, no. About the other thing. I'm not sure it's going on at all."

"Neither am I," said Arnold, a shade vehemently, I thought.

The Australian suddenly laughed out loud, and the girl joined in briefly before gazing wistfully at her empty glass. He caught the barman's eye and it was swiftly replenished. The barman looked a trifle weary.

"We could have a spread bet," Alfie suggested. "All you have to do is say when they'll go off together. High or low, 18 to 20 minutes? That'll make it more interesting."

Henry regarded him soberly. "I understand perfectly well how spread betting works, thank you, Alfred," he said. "Frankly, I'm not at all sure this is the sort of thing we should be joking about, and I'm far from convinced that the scenario is as you imagine. But you'll only think me a killjoy, so I'll wager a round of drinks they don't leave together at all."

"Bet struck," said Alfie, delightedly. "Arnold?"

Arnold gazed sadly into the middle distance. "I'll go above 20 minutes at 50p a minute, but I've got to get back to the garage," he said. "You've got to go high. When I came back from the Gents just now I overheard him talking about the days he flew 747s from Sydney to Singapore. And he's hardly touched that pint of lager."

This boy will go far, I thought. Even so. "What happens if you're right about the time it takes for the conversation to come around but he still says no?" I asked.

Arnold looked once more at the girl and then, bleakly, at me. "*No-one* would say no to that," he said, and walked out.

Some time later I paid a visit myself and caught a fragment of the conversation at the bar. She was drawing her index finger down the back of his hand, very lightly. "But I think everyone should take time out to relax, don't you? Especially on holiday," she was saying.

I glanced at the clock, which indicated that young Arnold was good for about £21 so far and I'd missed Powder River Grey. Seconds later a large Australian lady, burdened with parcels, strode into the bar and addressed her man from about 15 yards. "Mervyn! Give me a hand with these, will ya? Or are ya gonna sit there gabbin' all day? Bloody all right for some!"

I wouldn't say the girl moved as fast as Linford Christie but then, in fairness, her clothes were tighter. I turned to Alfie. "Now then," I said. "I'll have a £20 win double that these two *do* go off together and it'll happen within the next two minutes. Bet struck?"

"Oh, very funny," he said. "Very droll. By the way, that Pritchard-Gordon thing got beat by the Geoff Lewis nag you mentioned. You could have had the forecast. Looks like nobody wins."

Henry cleared his throat. "Ah. Sorry, old man. As you know, I thought it unseemly to speculate on the young lady's, um, profession. I merely said that she and the Australian gentleman would not leave this establishment together. I believe I was correct in this. In other words, it's your round."

"Pandofell! Ascot Gold Cup! Lester Piggott up!" Brendan shouted.

Alfie got them in, as good as gold. I must have returned to the old obsession again because he quite startled me when he spoke. "What a rum do, eh? What do you make of it all?"

"What? Oh, I don't know. I expect Gavin will run it off 7st 10lb in that six furlong Goodwood nursery. That's what he normally does. I'll ring him up if you like," I said.

fifteen

Martin Pipe – An Appreciation

Few things are certain in racing, but it is reasonable to suppose that Martin Pipe will go on breaking records for as long as he holds a trainer's licence.

He is an obsessive, of course, and I doubt that he will mind anyone saying that. It would be impossible to maintain his standards of excellence without living and breathing the sport every minute of the day. He drives himself hard, and maybe he drives others as well. It is unwise to be on the wrong side of him. He acknowledged as much when including the words "Am I That Difficult?" in a race title at a meeting he sponsored not long ago in the West Country.

Chester Barnes once told me a wonderful story about Pipe. Apparently the pair of them started playing table tennis in the afternoons, with the trainer almost certainly unaware of Barnes's impressive record at international level. Not surprisingly, the score was often 21-0.

"He kept saying I should have a handicap," recalled Barnes. "I had to use a bat which had worn completely smooth on both sides, and when that didn't help him I played with one which had no handle. In the end, the only way to make it close was to use a bottle with a deep punt in its base. The ball flew all over the place, and sometimes we had to retrieve it from the rafters in the barn.

We were helpless with laughter. Then, the next thing I knew, there were a hundred horses here and the games stopped."

I like Martin Pipe. The main reason is that there is no side to him. Introduced to people at the races, he will make time for them and listen to what they have to say, even if he is on his way to saddle four in the same race.

The media labels him 'difficult' because he does not comply with requests for detailed future plans (and that will never change), but in other respects he is the most approachable of men. He has the common touch, a quality not always apparent among his colleagues.

Although it looked harmless, knockabout stuff at the time, Pipe's interview with Desmond Lynam after Miinnehoma had won the Grand National was very revealing. Lynam, not easily fazed, was disconcerted to find the trainer still talking to owner Freddie Starr on his mobile when the interview started. Ninety-nine per cent of interviewees would have switched the machine off, but Pipe said all he had to say to Starr before turning to Lynam again.

You can call that unreasonable, even rude, if you want. But Pipe is not interested in fame, and not particularly interested in the requirements of the media either. Lynam is a famous personality, but Pipe treated him exactly the way he would have treated a local radio reporter. (And quite right, too.) In either case, talking to the man who pays the bills would have come first. Try to imagine anything or anyone coming between Jenny Pitman and a Desmond Lynam interview.

There is no point in being an obsessive unless you do it properly. Like Lester Piggott, Pipe acts first and fields questions later. If you suggest that leaving the top-weight in a valuable hurdle at the overnight stage, thereby helping a stable-companion by keeping a handful of runners out of the handicap, is not in the spirit of the rules as they stand, he will give you a pained look. "Change the rules, then," he will say. He is not interested in a nicey-nicey game of soldiers. He is interested in winning. If you're worried about putting a horse in a claimer because Pipe or one of his people may be lurking, don't put it in. It's quite simple, really.

"Horses come here to improve," he once told me. "A decent horse may become a champion (Make A Stand being the best example), one with a bit of ability may win a good race, and a bad horse may win *something*." If you see Pipe with a group of owners who have just won a Taunton seller with a confirmed plodder, his joy is unconfined. There is no apparent difference between his happiness levels at Newton Abbot and Aintree.

He is a genius as surely as Piggott was. I have had the privilege of interviewing them both on a number of occasions, and the number of times they introduced any subject other than racing into the conversation could be counted on the fingers of one hand. (Especially as Lester's tally stands at zero; at least MCP talks engagingly about his favourite restaurant in Brixham.)

Do not underestimate his dead-pan humour. Once, when we were sitting in the kitchen at Pond House, talking about his Saturday piece for *The Sporting Life*, I naïvely suggested that one of his runners in the Midlands Grand National was poorly handicapped with one of David Nicholson's. Quick as a flash, he looked across at Chester Barnes and said, "Better take that horse out, Ches. Ian says it can't win."

How long will he go on? Hard to say, really, although I believe it would rankle with him until they day they send for the long box if he retired without winning the Cheltenham Gold Cup. Maybe, when it finally happens (which it will), he'll use the occasion to hand over to son David. It's not the sort of thing you ask him, though. Not if you want to spend any more time in the kitchen.

sixteen

In Arcadia

There are people working in betting offices now who do not remember the 'sound only' days, and therefore cannot imagine how business was conducted. In the debate about what is on offer these days – much of it contributing to bookmakers' profits without returning anything to racing – we should try to work out what might have happened if nothing had changed.

Betting shops, legalised in 1960, did good business when there were only two meetings an afternoon, with longish gaps between races. Commentaries were provided by Exchange Telegraph, any number of horses used to finish fast without quite getting there, and punters had to use their own imagination, often blaming jockeys they couldn't see.

When meetings were lost to the weather, there would sometimes be coverage of the trotters from Vincennes or Steerebeek. And people would bet. Even though the result was announced in sudden-death fashion, and there was no commentary, people would bet. From then on, sensible bookmakers knew that punters could be tempted by events which were literally foreign to them. The idea that more than a tiny percentage of betting office punters are prepared to specialise is fanciful nonsense, and anyone who doubts it should simply go along and observe for an hour or two.

Clichés are tiresome, but often accurate enough. Betting offices are a licence to print money, which is why Coral eagerly snapped up the Arthur Prince chain and Ladbrokes wanted the whole lot. Or look at the way Fred Done has expanded far beyond his beloved Manchester to take in cities as far afield as Bristol. Sure, smaller independent outlets have closed and there aren't as many betting offices as there used to be, but then, there aren't as many corner shops, either. Big embraces little, or forces it out of business.

Pictures arrived in 1987, and I presented for the first four years on SIS. It doesn't really matter who presents – Ian Carnaby, Des Lynam, Robert DeNiro – because the punters are generally pointing the other way. Offer an opinion and any self-respecting betting office regular will ask why you're not sunning yourself in the Bahamas, then. The betting, the race, the returns; nothing else matters. It's a great pity, because SIS has some excellent broadcasters, professional enough – even after all these years – to call a 'virtual' race without a hint of boredom or tell us that ball 33 is 'hot' at the moment.

Anyway, the pictures arrived and betting offices spruced themselves up, becoming much cleaner and more comfortable without, of course, attracting women – which was, is, and always will be an outright non-starter. But would the pictures themselves, once the novelty wore off, be enough to keep a younger audience interested? If the answer to that is "no," we must accept that the hard-bitten characters who go back as far as 1960 would gradually have dropped off the perch and betting offices would have called it a day. It really is as straightforward as that.

Thus, no matter what they may have said at the time, the best thing that ever happened to off-course bookmakers was the advent of the Lottery. Because, in search of their Holy Grail, the oft-quoted 'level playing field', they were in a position not merely to agitate for lucky numbers, Rapido and the rest of it, but to build on that and introduce roulette and virtual racing gadgetry to sit alongside the coyly-named Amusement With Prizes machines.

Thus, betting offices became the arcades we have today … and youngsters with change in their pockets have always loved arcades. We mustn't call it exploitation, of course. But that's precisely what it is.

seventeen

Feeling Good In Finchley

When Zoman was beaten a short head by Opera House at the Curragh in 1992, I thought it might be a good idea to find out what life was like a few yards back from the edge. You could say I needed Zoman to win that day. If your biggest bets are the ones designed to get you out of trouble, there is a flaw in the overall plan. I use the word 'plan' loosely, of course.

The story of the American gambler who pauses outside a casino and says, "Jeez, I hope I break even tonight: I could use the money" is probably apocryphal. Only other gamblers understand it, anyway. Never tell risqué jokes in mixed company, and never have gambling conversations with non-gamblers. You may come across as a bit of a character, but no-one wants to change places.

Pulling back from the edge means fewer celebrations, fewer conversations with complete strangers. But '92 was a watershed year. The year I realised that five or six winners would have to appear on the same piece of paper for me to force a draw. And I was never really into accumulators.

1987 was rather different. That was the year quite a lot of people wanted me to work for them. SIS and Extel, who were vying to broadcast pictures to the betting shops, needed a presenter, John Sanderson needed a marketing man, and the *London Daily News* needed a racing correspondent. So I chose

Robert Maxwell and his brand new 24-hour London paper, which was really going to give the *Evening Standard* something to think about. And probably did, for the five months it lasted.

I'd interviewed Maxwell a couple of times for the BBC, around the time he was trying to merge Oxford United and Reading. "What do you think of the name Thames Valley Royals?" he asked. "Sounds like a big box of biscuits," I replied, so it was probably just as well he didn't know who he was getting for a racing correspondent.

Anyway, the *London Daily News* folded, the compensation took a while to come through, I owed two of the big four bookmakers a few bob, and Ken Oliver, who'd recruited me for the paper and went on to work for *The Guardian*, said we really ought to have a drink in Fleet Street. Good idea, I said. I was already due to see some former Extel colleagues in Finchley at lunchtime, and the day began to take shape.

Like most racing people, I was following the Steve Cauthen v Pat Eddery title race very closely. Nearly 15 years later John Hanmer, Steve's agent, told me he'd backed his man quite heavily, as had others close to the camp. Perhaps that was why the American ended up riding in Edinburgh claimers in early November.

Steve Cauthen and John Hanmer

But I didn't think he could win on Infanta de Castile that afternoon. My one strength is the ability to differentiate between modest form and poor form, and I knew that the filly's recent placed effort at a Grade 1 track – which guaranteed favouritism here – meant very little. Hopping Around, on the other hand, had been running well enough on the northern circuit and Chris Thornton had engaged Pat to ride him.

I reasoned that one of the firms would take £250 and the other £200, and both bets were struck at 7'2. For some reason – part of the brain may have been gearing up for a long day – I went out of the Finchley pub and had another £50 on him in cash. I had no desire to hear the race. The Extel lads arrived, we had a few jars, they went away again. I sat there for quite a while, taking it as a bad sign that there was no telephone call to the pub – pre-mobile days, you see – though they'd have needed Yellow Pages for the number.

The bet itself was hardly my biggest, but both accounts would be clear. On the other hand, a thousand each would take some finding. Looking sideways at the screen from the betting office door, all I wanted to see was two words, not one or three. And there *were* two, and the first one began with 'H', and I couldn't recall any other H's in the race. Finally it could only be Hopping Around, and it was. And I'd never really spent time in Finchley before – The Flask in Hampstead and the Galtymore Dance Club in Cricklewood, yes, of course – but not Finchley. A fine borough, I must say, bathed in late autumn sunshine. I admired it all the way to Swiss Cottage, and then all the way back, having remembered the fifty in cash.

One takes a taxi on such occasions, but Ken had gone by the time I reached the Cheshire Cheese. I can never quite recall the early evening on days like these, but obviously there was the Cheese followed by the White Swan in Fetter Lane when it was still one of the great Fleet Street watering holes. Indeed, it features prominently in Anne Robinson's autobiography.

Gamblers celebrate any sort of recovery. We lose ten units, win seven, and call it a draw. The things we get right were always bound to happen, and the things we get wrong were bad luck or pilot error. "The highway is for gamblers, better use your sense. Take what you have gathered from coincidence," as Bob Dylan sang. Not that Hopping Around was a coincidence. Three days later he finished sixth in the November Handicap, so he must have been a good thing at Edinburgh. I remember him with great affection.

All that remained was a quiet spaghetti in Frith Street and a game of blackjack in Charlie Chester's. I couldn't really lose, because the accounts were square and I had only £200 in cash on me. They're not all that keen when you look relaxed. The £200 became £1,800, but they don't really like you nodding off, either, so they got me a taxi to the Astor Court behind the BBC, where I used to stay when I thought I'd end up presenting Grandstand.

I woke up the next morning with £50 notes all over the bed, which should happen to everyone at least once. I can't remember what happened after that, but no doubt I found a way of giving some back. The form-book suggests as much.

eighteen

Still California Split For Me

Racing has not fared particularly well in the cinema, although I nurse a certain affection for *The Yellow Rolls Royce*, in which Rex Harrison discovers his wife 'in flagrante' with the chauffeur in the Ascot car park. Not quite 'in flagrante delicto', it's true, although we all know how long it takes to run the Gold Cup.

The best racing picture is, I think, *The Killing* (1956) because the racecourse scenes where Sterling Hayden tries to organise a two million dollar heist are entirely authentic. There is nothing glossy about it – the track is grey and functional, the thieves grimly determined, the atmosphere claustrophobic. I like the 'all or nothing' feel to it because those are the only bets that matter in the end.

Eight Men Out (1988) deals with bribes taken by the Chicago White Sox baseball team to lose the 1919 World Series. It is popularly supposed to have given birth to the saying "Say It Ain't So, Joe", although this actually related to Joe DiMaggio's retirement many years later. *Eight Men Out* was beautifully filmed, with outstanding baseball sequences.

Critics dismissed *The Gambler* (1974) as sub-Freudian fodder about a college professor with a will to lose, but I thought James Caan – way over the top in other pictures – caught the anti-hero just right. He punishes his mother on the tennis court before asking her for money, relaxes with his girlfriend when his football selections are miles ahead at half-time (no need to fill you in on the outcome there) and memorably tells the dealer to give him the three when holding 18 at blackjack. And it is a three, of course, because that kind of invincibility exists for a second or two now and then in a gambler's life.

But the best scene in *The Gambler* sees a sympathetic bookmaker, played by Paul Sorvino, trying to buy Caan some time with the bookies he owes. And they just don't care that he's a college professor, and has read books they've never even heard of. He's a loser, and he owes, and they don't send polite letters.

The Hustler (1961), which is bleak, and *The Cincinnatti Kid* (1965), rather more easy-going, have much to recommend them, though the Kid holding a house of aces against Lancey's straight flush with only two of them playing takes a bit of swallowing. I preferred the low-budget *Desert Hearts* (1986), parts of which are set in a seedy Reno casino, where it soon becomes apparent that Helen Shaver, in town for a quick divorce, has rather more chance with the beautiful dealer Patricia Charbonneau than any of the local lads has. Tastefully done, with a proper small-town America feel to it, and an Ella Fitzgerald soundtrack.

Wandering around Bristol the other day, I heard Richard Harris's 'MacArthur Park' on the radio. I'd have bet the house to a grand that the DJ wouldn't let it finish, because records which go on for seven minutes plus are a non-starter these days. That would have been a very safe investment, with the win double a bonus when he made the inevitable crass remark afterwards.

I don't pretend to understand 'MacArthur Park' – "Someone left the cake out in the rain. I don't think that I can take it, 'cos it took so long to bake it, and I'll never have that recipe again", etc, and I dare say it's pretentious, but the writer Jimmy Webb put a hundred times more thought into it than anything you hear today. It's also quite beautiful in its own way, the old men playing chequers by the trees conjuring up some rustic Arthurian scene. Harris had just had a hit with Camelot in the West End, of course.

He made some real duds for the silver screen, but was magnificent in the late Lindsay Anderson's *This Sporting Life* (1963), easily the best British film about professional sport ever made. Harris plays Frank Machin, an ex-miner who achieves fame as a rugby league player but is too crude and violent to win over his landlady, the widowed and embittered Rachel Roberts. The way the crowd, so recently adulatory, turns against Machin as his self-destructive streak and hopeless quest take their toll on the pitch is almost sickeningly real. I doubt that modern audiences could sit through it.

All of which leaves us with Robert Altman's infinitely lighter *California Split* (1974), in which Elliott Gould and George Segal gamble their way from racetrack to all-night casino to early-morning poker game, with Segal eventually getting them out of trouble right at the death. As I have written before, *California Split* is extremely funny and captures gambling types perfectly – the way complete strangers talk like long lost brothers at the races, for example.

But only a gambler like Altman could know that, in almost any pairing, one player is committed to the game – the way of life – for its own sake, while the other, in this case Segal, will draw a line under it and head back to the real world. Soiled suit, bleary eyes and some strange looks in the office, but ultimate safety. Good old boring safety. It's a marvellous film which, sadly, is seen only rarely on British television these days.

nineteen

Halfway To Aintree

Young Albie, who is 53, wants to go to Aintree. "I've never seen the Grand National live, and you know your way around," he said.

Well, this is perfectly true. My version of Billy Fury's 'Halfway to Paradise', performed only a few hours before Hallo Dandy's triumph in 1984, is still discussed in Birkenhead, though I have not revisited the nightclub in question.

Young Albie is betting again, but only small. His dad, Old Albie, was a fearless punter and no mean crooner in his day. There was only one thing about him which irritated people slightly, and that was a tendency to finish off their sentences with lyrics from popular songs. He couldn't help himself.

If some poor soul suffered an agonising, short-head defeat in the Mecca shop in Crawford Street W1, then rallied bravely and muttered, "Just one of those things," Old Albie would nod sympathetically and say, "A trip to the moon on gossamer wings. Just one of those things".

In the end he had to go, because not everyone appreciated his fine rendition of Al Bowlly's 'The Very Thought Of You', especially when the first at Hackney was due off.

Young Albie does not sing, but is deeply into quizzes. He fires questions at you all the time. "Name the only mare in modern times to have produced two Grand National winners." (Be honest, you haven't a clue, have you? I might just as well have asked you about bus routes in downtown Rangoon.)

Miss Alligator was the dam of both Red Alligator and Anglo. I only know this because Red Alligator in 1968 was the last time I backed the winner, and Young Albie asked me the same question several years ago, when his dad was singing 'Here's That Rainy Day' in the corner of the Alpino restaurant in Marleybone High Street. It was rather apt, too, because when we went outside it was pouring.

"Who was supposed to ride Highland Wedding in 1969, before Eddie Harty took over?"

"Owen McNally."

"Blimey. No one knows that. How come you remember it?"

"Well, Owen McNally was a bit of a job jockey, and I followed people like that from a very early age. I was fascinated by them. You could say Owen McNally was the Vince Slattery *de son époque*," I said, feeling quite pleased with myself.

"Eh?"

"Doesn't matter. Two out of three, Albie. Ask me another."

"Have you met anyone famous at Aintree?"

I thought hard. The fact is, I worked with Judith Chalmers on BBC Radio once. And David Icke came up and introduced himself. "Hello, mate," he said. Just like that. I think this may have been before that funny spell when he thought he was the Chosen One.

I always wondered about that. He was a goalie, David Icke. I suppose, if you were the centre-half in his team, about to nod the ball away, you'd get out of the way pretty sharpish if he shouted, "Mine!" Divine intervention, see. You'd certainly expect him to catch it, too.

I was a goalie, but I've never been chosen for anything.

"Is that it?" Albie said. "Judith Chalmers and David Icke? No one from the world of stage and screen?"

I cast back in my memory. "Frank Windsor," I said. "He was there once. He walked past the radio scanner but I'd had quite a big bet in the handicap hurdle and missed him. You remember Frank Windsor. He played John Watt in *Z Cars* and *Softly, Softly*. Stratford Johns was always giving him a hard time."

"What does he do now?" Albie asked.

"Well, you know when you're watching Channel 4 Racing on midweek afternoons? He comes on in between and advertises life policies for the over 50s. It goes on for ever. He sits on the edge of the table and looks deadly serious and says it's time to think about those 'final expenses'. Just when you're trying to solve a tricky sprint handicap. I liked him better in *Z Cars*. It's all a bit of a downer, but apparently no salesman will call and you get a free carriage clock."

'What, so you can count yourself down?" Albie said. "What are these 'final expenses' anyway?"

"Search me. I can't imagine any expenses being final. I thought they just went round in a sort of loop. I was going to leave some cash in the drawer and let the council, the Inland Revenue and Wilson Sports & Racing divide it up. But I suppose he means the box and everything."

"Good grief. I hope we don't bump into him at Aintree," Albie said. "Anyway, let's have a drink. The Alpino has closed, but I know a small hotel."

"With a wishing well?" I murmured, innocently, but Young Albie was already striding on ahead. I think I may have heard his dad chuckle though.

twenty

Zarzuela – Short Story, 2003

The girl is small and dark and heavy-breasted. About 19, and says her name is Conchita. Not that I've ever heard a tom call herself by her real name.

Certainly not the ones Lennie fixed up in Shepherd Market, or the college girls who asked for a job in Kentish Town. He 'looked after' a couple of parlours in the old days, when Voce and I went round for the take. Or Lennie's share of it, anyway. They were clean and properly run, with a discreet door out the back. "Know why the punters always come back?" he said to me once. "It's because they never hear what the toms say when they've gone."

And he'd laugh his quiet, mirthless laugh as the brisk, joyless encounter helped put his daughters through college somewhere many miles away. You didn't ask Lennie about things like that.

Conchita finishes things off expertly enough. There's no hard glitter yet, but it'll come. I pay over the odds, because I'll probably want to come back if I think it's safe. Safe. Secure. Not words I use very often. To be honest I've taken one or two chances lately. You do in the end, as Harper said. You forget the rules you've made for yourself, and then it's all over quite quickly. But it's been nearly two years now, and I'm starting to think it'll be all right.

I come back via Calle de Viriato, crossing Rafael and skirting Quevedo to the south. The sun is over the Parque del Oeste, still searingly hot. *Tres meses de infierno,* as the madrilenos say. Three months of hell. But this is the right place to be. They think of Spain, but they never think of Madrid. One day, when no-one cares any more, I'll have a second-storey walk-up in Pavones, with an old crone for the bare essentials. This is what I tell myself.

———————

"Señor Maioranos." The waiter bowed and left the bill on the immaculate white tablecloth. Venancio glanced at it without interest. He used to drink a single fino before dinner, with maybe a couple of glasses of the Marques to follow. Nowadays he spent more time at the bar, and drank three finos before sitting down. It was harder to work it off at 50, but he punished himself steadily.

Venancio seldom came to Madrid in summer. When he did, he endured the small army of sweating, ill-informed tourists and stood before the Goyas in the Prado. From light to darkness. From the early cartoons to the Pinturas Negras, with their scenes of witchcraft, suffering and death. He would contemplate The Sabbath for minutes on end, then sit in a cool, quiet bar off the Calle Veronica, sipping his first fino of the day.

Perhaps he should have joined one of the great sherry houses. He often thought so, but was not given to regret for the past. An elegant man of impeccable taste, except where rough trade was concerned, he no longer needed work. It was a question of choosing the right moment, tidying things up properly and moving on. He had never been to South America, never seen Corcovado or the wide, impressive boulevards of Santiago de Chile.

He was tired, and tired men made mistakes. He paid the bill and set off for Chueca. It was too loud, too garish for him these days, but chance encounters there were anonymous enough. It was surprising how many of the boys were Brazilian. It made him think of Rio even more.

———————

I go out to Moncloa and beyond. Some of the British jockeys used to come and ride at Zarzuela. It was a good place to be when the air cooled late in the evening, and the lights went on over Madrid.

You could just sit there with a beer, watching people. I went through a spell when I tried to follow the Spanish form, but it was too complicated. I needed Janie for that. Not that she ever studied the form all that much, she just watched the horses and jockeys.

"See the ones talking to each other as they come out?" she said at Windsor one night. "If you get up close, it's always about cars or women. They don't give a toss. It's the quiet ones I like, the ones who don't say anything at all. They know they've got to get it right." Anything she said was all right with me.

It doesn't do any good, thinking about these things. I don't know where she went when it all blew up, although Dundee was probably favourite. Jute City, as she used to say. She'd have loved Zarzuela, especially the tapas bar opposite the big old crumbling stands. That was where the trainers and jocks went afterwards. Bloody deafening for a couple of hours. Celebrations, recriminations, all the rest of it. Same in any language.

The first time I saw Janie, she was singing 'I'm Old Fashioned' in the Talbot off Holland Road. She had long auburn hair, a tight top which did the right things, and a leather skirt which had cost enough. I thought she was with the band, then realised she just got up and did a number now and then. Maybe she knew the saxophonist, because he glanced at her and they did a moody 'Cry Me A River'. It was hard to imagine her crying that much over anyone, though.

I didn't meet Lennie Miles that night, or Voce, or any of them. But I went in the Talbot quite a bit in those days. I suppose I was trying to turn things round after coming out. Sometimes you make a minor change and it wrongfoots people. I could have gone back to Woodford or Leyton or anywhere over there, where they all turn round as soon as a copper comes in and everything goes quiet, but I didn't want that. You do your two years and that's it. Some of the old cons would ramble on all afternoon, comparing this nick and that, perks they'd got, bent screws, all the rest of it. And none of them were ever going back, until one day you'd come in and realise you hadn't seen them for a while, and the barman would shake his head slowly when you asked, and that was it.

So I went across London and found a little place in Shepherds Bush and did casual work for people who didn't need references.

I'd been a careful thief – a *good* thief, never greedy – for a long time; posh Jewish houses up the Bishops Avenue mainly, always working alone and never hanging around too long. When they finally had me it was only because they were chasing someone else, a bloody fluke really, but I never talk about luck. I was a thief with a good fence in Luton, I looked after the money, and that's why I've got some sort of chance. It was never enough for the little place I wanted, not even nearly, but it was enough to have me thinking along those lines. And that's how I came to hear Janie singing 'Cry Me A River', and wanted to hear her again.

Venancio was putting off the call to Ramon, even though he was bound to make it eventually. But not this afternoon. He walked along Calle Alcala and into the Museo Taurino, with its six remaining bulls' heads. Manolete's pink and gold outfit was also on display, together with the blood transfusion equipment they used, unavailingly, on the fateful day in 1947 when he was gored.

Venancio did not regard himself as an expert on the corrida. But, in a life otherwise devoid of close attachments, he had spent a few weeks with a young torero in Aranjuez, hearing his lover's name chanted rapturously by the crowd after a clean kill – and they were all clean. The relationship lasted a while and faded away properly. Discretion was never a problem for Venancio, but Felipe lived in fear of exposure. So it ended quietly and with regret on both sides, and Venancio went back to arrangements which were brief and strictly business.

He strolled back across the bullring and sat high up on the shimmering steps. Not calling Ramon today would be a further sign that concentration and self-discipline were slipping. He closed his eyes and thought of Manolete waiting patiently for death, with panic all around.

I think I'd have been happy, just earning a bit here and there and listening to the jazz. But it's always a mistake to think you've made a fresh start, especially when all you've done is move across town. The next time I went in the Talbot, a few things were different.

For a start, Janie was talking to an immaculately dressed man who turned out to be Lennie Miles. And there was a hanger-on with them, too, an ex-con who recognised me and nodded across the room. So it was no great surprise when Lennie and his £800 suit came and sat down.

There's always one chance to walk away. I knew Lennie's reputation and I wasn't about to get involved. He wouldn't have minded that. As Harper once told me, it's only *after* you start working for him that you can't get away. But he had Janie with him, and she smiled and said hello in a way that was all right, and I saw that she was nearer 35 than the 25 I'd originally thought, and I didn't mind that at all. The main reason to walk away was that she so obviously belonged to Lennie.

He gave me a card, which I put away knowing I'd never ring the number. Even now I can't tell you why he was interested, although he probably knew I'd done bird without talking or moaning about it. He liked people who kept quiet. When I thought about it again and agreed to drive for him, I discovered he listened to classical music, Brahms as often as not, and often said nothing for hours on end.

But he was into everything. Clip joints, massage parlours, escort agencies, illegal gambling dens, short-term loans. Sometimes the last two went hand in hand, which was why there was always plenty of muscle around the place. It was almost as if he hated human weakness so much he had to punish it. The underground casino he ran – or Voce ran – off the Hackney Road wasn't even bent. It didn't need to be. There were Chinese and Greeks in there from 4am to noon, or whenever their restaurants opened, or the first race was due off. They worked and gambled, worked and gambled, and then one day that was it, because they were in hock for more than they could ever find, so they disappeared, or tried to. In a way, and although I didn't like myself for it, I understood Lennie's contempt.

I sat outside all these places, because that was the deal. I drove him round in the Merc, and sometimes Janie was there, but that was it. And I earned more in a month than I'd have picked up in a year in Shepherds Bush.

The other thing Lennie couldn't stand was south London, even though he was born there. Streatham and Brixton were where he and Voce put the bite on people in the early days – small-time protection and the like. Sometimes I watched Voce without him noticing. He was massive – huge shoulders and crinkly black hair, like Victor Mature, but more Slav looking. He could run a six-inch blade across his knuckles like a three-card trickster teasing a deck of cards, and his baby-blue eyes sometimes filled with hate. I had a feeling he liked boys. The story was that he and Lennie nearly killed a rival gang leader once and Voce went down for it, so Lennie looked after him from then on.

That was what the boys said, anyway. But they didn't know much about Janie, except that Lennie had taken her out of some Glasgow dive where she sang and spent a bit of time with the punters. Like I say, Lennie hated the way people carried on, but he always got something out of it.

About six months on, I noticed a change. He let trusted members of the firm handle the ongoing business and started concentrating on property deals, redevelopments and the rest of it. He sought meetings with local councillors and politicians, no doubt offering them sweeteners along the way. We started to see less of him.

"I'm going up north for a while. Look after Janie. Take her to the races, she likes that," he said one night in the Talbot. Janie seemed fifty-fifty about it, but Lennie's ideas were more like instructions. He left us the Merc.

We did everything that summer. Boat trips to Windsor every Monday, Yarmouth and the fairground and the dogs afterwards, endless days in Brighton with all the old characters stuck in a time-warp, even an open-top bus trip to the Derby. And as the days went by, so she lost that hard, self-protective edge and told me bits and pieces about the past, though never very much about her childhood.

One night we went back to the Talbot and she sang 'I Wished On The Moon' and told me that Dorothy Parker had written the words. And I must have looked pretty blank, because I didn't know Dorothy Parker from the woman who sold papers on the corner of Oxford Street, so she teased me and gave me the poor old Tommy treatment. And I thought that was a bit rich, because she could give me at least five years, but she dug me in the ribs in the playful way they do when you can have the rest if you really want it. And I really did.

It all started that night, and I wasn't nearly enough for her, of course. But I had the feeling that no one had ever held her when it was all over before, and that helped. I remember every second of it, even waking up first and remembering we were going to Salisbury. And then wondering, only a moment or two later, whether there might come a day when Salisbury wouldn't be nearly far enough.

Venancio wished he'd seen Maria Callas in her prime at La Zarzuela in 1958. Light opera had never interested him all that much, although the current production of La Dolorosa was all right. He rang Ramon afterwards.

"Is it done?"

"Not yet."

"Are there problems?"

"Not at all. Leave it with me."

Not at all. Venancio pondered the words. There were no problems with the job, of course. In Madrid, it always started with the phone call from Ramon, then the photograph. Sometimes the photograph was old and faded, a newspaper shot reproduced a hundred times. But that hardly mattered, because Venancio never started from scratch. Ramon was contacted by the client, and it was Ramon who made the initial inquiries. He looked after receptionists and barmen, building up a network of contacts. It cost money, but in Ramon's line of work that was all right.

Venancio picked up an envelope at Atocha station, and the single strip of paper inside gave him the address of a hotel on the Plaza de Santa Ana. In Venancio's experience the information was often out of date, but much depended on how long the subject had been on the move. In this case, Ramon said it was a couple of years, which was encouraging. And after watching the third floor hostel for three hours, Venancio saw the Englishman come down the steps and cross the square.

He had killed 17 men in his time, all with clinical efficiency. There was nothing personal in it, apart from the first time, when someone tried to blackmail him in Jerez. Venancio was relaxed, courteous, civil and entirely amoral. It was simply a matter of being patient, allied to the element of surprise, often the quick knife on a dark street late at night. The people he killed did not take up much police time afterwards. Of the 17 victims, three had been living on their nerves for so long that fear was tinged with relief when they realised it was over at last. He was the perfect assassin, and therefore much in demand.

Janie stayed in regular touch with Lennie while he was away and, apart from that first night, always went back to the Maida Vale flat he'd set up for her. He trusted her, or so I thought.

When he was on his way home, I asked if she'd ever gamble on living abroad with me if I found the money. And she didn't quite laugh, but the hard edge came back and she said, "There's never enough money for something like that. And he'd kill us both. Get it straight. He gives you things. You don't take them from him. That's the way it is."

I left her at Maida Vale and went to the Kilburn office to wait for him. There was no small talk at all when he walked in, and he was white with anger. I thought at first that his new friends had let him down, but it was clearly more serious than that. Voce had left the running of the casino – which was important to Lennie if other things went wrong – to a Maltese who called himself Jimmy Feather and had quite a few hard cases at his beck and call. And Jimmy was on the take.

"Jimmy Feather stays in a pub called The Lamb in Beckenham," Lennie said. "He shacks up with the landlady there. Here are the directions. Go and sort it out, Voce. He never comes anywhere near Hackney again."

I didn't like any of this. "Let's not forget I'm just the driver," I said.

And he swung round and stared at me. "Are you?" he said. "Are you really? Just the driver? Well, you'd better fucking drive then, hadn't you?"

Sometimes, sitting in Zarzuela a couple of years later, I can see I played it badly. I should have got ahead of Voce and driven off by myself. It wouldn't have prevented what happened to Janie, but Jimmy Feather would still be alive. As it was, once Voce was in the car, I hadn't a prayer. Voce was stupid and vicious, but totally loyal to Lennie. He'd have killed me to keep Lennie sweet.

It was midnight on a Sunday and the pub was in darkness. I heard him rattling the door and saw a light go on upstairs. Maybe Jimmy had had a few drinks, because he'd never have opened the door otherwise. Or maybe he thought it was his woman. The rest happened very quickly, but Voce got in and finished him in a blind rage. The woman wasn't in there, but it must have been her pulling up on the forecourt in a blaze of lights as Voce came running out.

No-one who shacked up with Jimmy Feather would be likely to panic, and she certainly didn't. It was my fault for cutting the lights on the Merc, because it meant she could pick out the number easily enough. Sizing things up, she suddenly swung full circle and drove off. Voce said to go after her, but I'm a thief, not a killer. I rang Lennie and he sounded strangely calm, maybe thinking she'd rely on gangland retribution. A fair call, but his biggest ever mistake. When we got back to Hackney, Harper and his friends were already there. They'd followed Lennie from the moment he got back to London.

"The point is," Harper said, "You only went down there on Lennie Miles' instructions. Voce would never have thought of it, and you're only the driver".

"Lennie just said to sort it out. He didn't tell Voce to kill him."

"Oh, come on, Tommy boy. Voce damn nearly killed a man in Streatham ten years ago, and that was only because Miles lost it completely."

"But he hasn't actually killed anyone."

"He's an accessory to murder, and so are you. I don't care about Voce, who's certain to go down anyway, and I don't care a fiddler's fuck about you. But I haven't left that filthy dive in Hackney alone for five years for nothing. I want Lennie Miles out of harm's way for a long, long time, and you're going to help me."

"I don't think so. I'm no grass."

"No, of course you're not. You're just a pathetic tea leaf, in way over your head. But let's see if this puts a different slant on things." And he reached into his pocket and pulled out a photograph, which was of Janie trying to cover her face, but without success. There was a livid gash from somewhere up near her ear to the corner of her mouth. The blood had not congealed for very long.

"Have a little think, Tommy. Just bear in mind, he cut her only an hour or so before sending Voce out to kill Feather. Voce let Feather run the casino for a while as a thank-you for laying on a couple of rent boys. Voce can't do it but he likes watching, know what I mean? But someone told Lennie that Feather was milking the casino, and that same someone let him know about you and the Glasgow tart. Know why he wanted you at the races? He was setting up a couple of bent bookies to launder drugs money a few months down the line, and you'd have known your way around by then. Not quite as straightforward as thieving, is it?"

We cut the deal on a park bench overlooking the Thames by Hammersmith Bridge. I didn't want to go into any sort of programme organised by Harper. From what I'd heard it was nearly always Canada, and I couldn't face it. All I wanted was a passport and a new identity. If I thought giving evidence would bring me closer to Janie I was a bloody fool, because she just retreated into herself and then disappeared altogether. Back to Jute City, some said. But I sent Lennie down for 10 years and Voce got twenty. When the judge had finished, Lennie just smiled at me and said, "Dead man."

Venancio watched the Englishman making small mistakes. If he was going to visit the puta again, he should be more careful in the streets behind Quevedo, where the lighting was poor. As for the racecourse at Zarzuela, that must be some sort of death wish. Venancio reflected grimly that he, too, had recently sat in a deserted arena after paying for sex.

"I have this feeling you're not going to do it," Ramon said.

"That is very perceptive of you."

"May I ask why? It's a lot of money."

"I can't say. Something about it isn't quite right. I'm a little tired. I need to be somewhere else for a while."

In fact, I need to be somewhere else all the time, he thought, although there was no need for Ramon to know that.

———————————

I sit on the steps of the Iglesia de San Isidro as the sun dips towards the Parque. Zarzuela suits me fine, but maybe it's time to look for somewhere in the south of the city. I'll do it today, and then work out another long trip, maybe all the way down to Brindisi before coming back to Pavones. There's just enough money for that.

You know, I've been pretty canny about things, really. The only time I ever said I'd like to live in Madrid was when Janie and I were in the La Tasca tapas bar off Warwick Avenue, and I'm pretty certain no-one took any notice.

I'm starting to think everything's all right now.

Index